KU-526-145

CREATIVE walls

CREATIVE walls

HOW TO DISPLAY AND ENJOY YOUR TREASURED COLLECTIONS

Geraldine James

CICO BOOKS

LONDON NEW YORK

Published in 2011 by
CICO Books
An imprint of Ryland Peters
& Small Ltd

20-21 Jockey's Fields
London WC1R 4BW

519 Broadway, 5th Floor
New York, NY 10012

www.cicobooks.com

10 9 8

Text © Geraldine James 2011
Design and photography ©
CICO Books 2011

ISBN 978 1 907563 15 7

For digital editions, visit
www.cicobooks.com/apps.php

The author's moral rights have been asserted.
All rights reserved. No part of this publication
may be reproduced, stored in a retrieval system, or
transmitted in any form or by any means, electronic,
mechanical, photocopying, or otherwise, without the
prior permission of the publisher.

A CIP catalog record for this book is available from
the Library of Congress and the British Library.

Printed in China

Editor: HELEN RIDGE
Designer: PAUL TILBY
Photographer: ANDREW WOOD
(pages 56, 57 by Sarah Bagner; pages 14, 15, 72, 73,
78, 79, 96, 97, 98, 99, 100, 101, 112, 113, 114, 116,
117, 124, 125, 126, 127, 130, 131, 142, 143, 144, 145,
204, 205 by Rick Haylor; page 211 by Jude Morgan)

CONTENTS

The blank wall gives the two small decorative pictures a sense of authority. The decorative details are provided by the jacquard fabric on the sofa and the lamp.

INTRODUCTION

It seems strange to get so excited about walls, but I do. FOR ME, A WALL IS A BEAUTIFUL BLANK CANVAS. A great big opportunity. I can't wait to get "painting." My paints are virtually anything I can find, or hang, or lean against that wall—photographs, art, ceramics, carvings, obscure curios discovered in bottom drawers, gorgeous objets unearthed in unlikely flea markets.

SOMETIMES A WALL IS BEAUTIFUL AS IT IS. FADED WALLPAPER CAN LOOK FANTASTIC. LAYERS OF PAINT REVEALED FOLLOWING CENTURIES OF DECORATION CAN BE A MESMERIZING WORK OF ART. Even fresh plaster itself—drying at different speeds to leave a rich patina of pinks—has a warm, lustrous appeal that a flat, white, painted wall can never match. COLD MINIMALISM HAS ITS PLACE, BUT NOT AT MY PLACE.

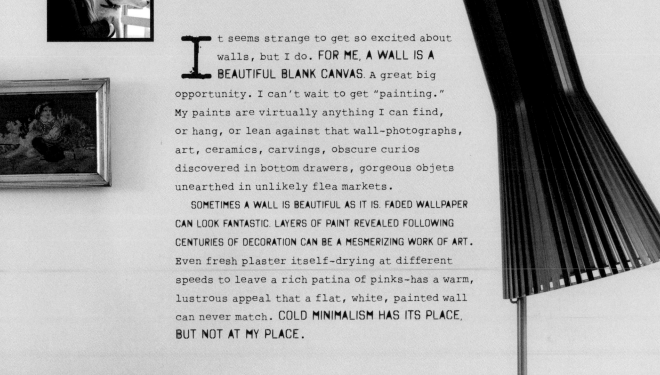

So does the world need a book about walls? Well, you can be the judge. All I know is that **A LOT OF PEOPLE ARE QUITE DAUNTED BY THAT BLANK CANVAS BEFORE THEM.** How do I hang photos? Which colors create a feeling of space? Should I go framed or frameless? Can I mix the two? Is it okay to hang plates?

In my day-to-day role as a buyer of interior décor, I'm always asked such questions. In fact

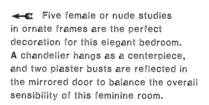 Five female or nude studies in ornate frames are the perfect decoration for this elegant bedroom. A chandelier hangs as a centerpiece, and two plaster busts are reflected in the mirrored door to balance the overall sensibility of this feminine room.

it has become something of an in-joke: "DOES MRS JAMES APPROVE?" The fact is what Mrs James thinks is irrelevant. You really don't need my approval or anyone else's. IF IT WORKS FOR YOU, IT WORKS. ANYTHING GOES. WELL, ALMOST. WE ALL HAVE A TASTE LIMIT. But what is key is creating walls that

↑ A jumbled selection of vintage pictures and frames adds a creative havoc to this boudoir-style bedroom. Perfume bottles and decorative scarves reflected in the huge mirror are the perfect mix for this comfortably eclectic room.

reflect you and your family and your personality. I'M ALWAYS AMAZED BY THE CREATIVITY DEMONSTRATED WITHIN PEOPLE'S HOMES. I regularly steal ideas for my own home and, inspired by a particular wall scheme, will set out to find similar art or artifacts that I can sell in my store (or often just keep for myself!).

To prove my theory that style is one hundred percent personal, THIS BOOK OFFERS A GLIMPSE INTO OTHER PEOPLE'S HOMES: friends, colleagues, friends of friends, friends of colleagues, all people who have been brave enough to take on a blank canvas and produce a stunning work of art. And there's the rub. To produce any art you have to be prepared to expose yourself to judgment, to opinion, to, dare I say it, the whims of fashion. You have to

This tall vintage railway sign is an unexpected decorative addition to to a stark white, modern bathroom.

TOILE

be confident enough to say, "THIS IS WHAT I BELIEVE IN, THIS IS WHAT I LIKE, THIS IS MY SOUL EXPOSED." The best art is the bravest art, when artists have dared to create something new or challenging rather than copy what already exists.

So MRS JAMES IS QUITE ADAMANT THAT THE WALLS YOU SEE IN THE FOLLOWING PAGES ARE NOT THERE TO BE COPIED. THEY ARE THERE TO PROVIDE INSPIRATION FOR YOUR OWN ARTISTIC JOURNEY. I don't believe in arbiters of taste. Of course, in everyday life we're surrounded by people telling us how to dress or how to style our homes, but if we all follow the advice of the so-called "experts" the world will be a very dull place. My walls, hopefully, show how varied and beautiful our homes can be. How AMAZING EFFECTS CAN BE ACHIEVED WITHOUT SPENDING VAST AMOUNTS OF MONEY OR EMPLOYING A TEAM OF INTERIOR DESIGNERS. How a basic understanding of simple design principles can help you overcome the physical limitations of space (a frustration we all face) and lead to a myriad of effects.

I'm not saying it's easy. It takes time and patience and, occasionally, a crazy obsession to find exactly the right frame in the right finish in the right color, but what you put in, you generally get out, and the results of your endeavors will be yours to enjoy every day.

MRS JAMES SAYS, "TRUST YOUR INSTINCTS AND GO FOR IT!"

Another clever idea for a bathroom—just because it's a bathroom, don't think you can't add your own decorative style. A vintage Venetian mirror is cleverly reflected into a mosaic glass mirror uniquely decorated with glass beads and ornaments.

CHAPTER 1
CLEVER IDEAS

I t's always tempting to go for the safe option when decorating our homes, even though IT'S SO EASY TO CREATE FASCINATING DISPLAYS with the simplest of objects, provided you put them together in a clever way. I hope this chapter will inspire you to be really open-minded and EXPERIMENT WITH THE SIMPLE BUT UNUSUAL— driftwood gathered from a river bank, concert tickets collaged in a frame, elegant script on a bare wall… the list is endless.

The owner's confident style shines through in this beautiful but simple bedroom, with a well-chosen verse in elegant script on the wall alongside a pair of naturally shed antlers, a vintage gown, and pure linen sheets.

Living with monochrome makes a bold graphic statement and gives the impression of modern masculinity.

Once you have made the move to monochrome, there's no looking back. Although a real commitment, it does make choosing things for the home much more focused because the framework is limited.

Although the carefully thought-out decoration of this light-filled New York apartment is predominantly monochrome, it is not at all hard-edged. The most striking feature is a floor-to-ceiling canvas destination board from a Melbourne tram, evoking memories of time spent in that city. Along with the soft toy on the desk, it's one of a number of objects with personal appeal dotted among fine designer pieces. Not only does this room say a lot about its owners, in particular their impeccable eye for design and detail, but it also offers an insight into what makes them tick.

▲ A beautiful glass lamp sits on a neat, well-organized office table. The uniform yellow pencils, probably used more as decoration than for writing, further illustrate the organized nature of the room and introduce a splash of color.

➡ Exquisitely chosen art and pictures give this home office a cool authority. The owners know exactly what they like and live a life surrounded by those elements. Everything is very considered and sophisticated, without being contrived, and the overall feel is one of comfort.

A young DJ, who divides his time between London and Manhattan, has a real magpie instinct. A collector of all things unusual, but definitely with a very masculine vibe, HE HAS USED THE WALLS OF HIS LONDON HOME IN HIS OWN, VERY INDIVIDUAL STYLE. I think that what he has done here is very inspiring. In setting up home on his own, he has succeeded in making a statement of trend without compromising on his individuality, and his confident authority shows through.

When buying items for your home, you need to visualize what they will look like in the intended location. This owner came across old metal signs and various discarded items and could picture them in his home. IT TOOK AN INSPIRED EYE TO SEE THAT THIS GASOLINE SIGN WOULD LOOK SUPERB ON THE WALL ABOVE THE BED.

◄ Although vintage, the gasoline sign over the bed gives a thoroughly modern and industrial feel, while battered old suitcases offer a unique bedside table. Combined with vintage shutters, this bedroom encapsulates the individual style of the owner.

↓ Picked up from the roadside, the chunk of marble hanging above a poisons cabinet, with a child's gas mask on top, tells us that the owner is not afraid to take a few decorating risks. The goldfish in a glass bowl represents a certain hominess in this quirky space.

Fixed to the wall opposite, a poster from a **1980**s advertising campaign fills the door in this seaside apartment. The two larger than life-size figures look as if they are about to enter the room.

➤ Favorite black-and-white photographs sit between the shower and closet, giving the space a sensual masculinity.

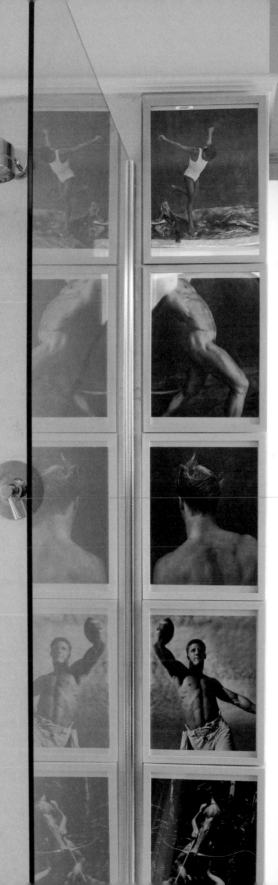

A subtle mural gives this bedroom with its awkward ceiling a unique fluid feel. The palette of warm colors and stream of broken light make the wall calm and easy on the eye

Shutters can be simply decorative but they can also have a practical purpose, such as hiding everyday objects that might otherwise jar in a tranquil space. On these pages, you can see examples of both in two very different locations.

In this bold, modern extension, which uses INDUSTRIAL FINISHES IN METAL AND CONCRETE, a bespoke frame was created for four identical vintage wooden shutters. They run the length of the wall, hiding unsightly everyday paraphernalia, such as the washing machine and refrigerator. WITH THEIR PEELING PAINT AND ANTIQUE FITTINGS, THE SHUTTERS HAVE ALSO GIVEN THE SPACE CHARACTER AND DEPTH, AND MADE IT ALTOGETHER QUITE HOMEY. The color of the shutters fits perfectly with the soothing neutral tones of the room. A flash of bright pink from the hydrangeas arranged casually in a stone bowl on a raw wood coffee table prevents those tones from becoming soporific.

SHUTTERS CAN ALSO BE USED PURELY AS WALL ART. An intimate still-life display of potted orchids flanked by table lamps is given the perfect textured backdrop by the wooden shutters fitted to the wall behind. The three panels echo the three elements of the still life and draw the eye to a display that might otherwise go unrecognized.

THE GORGEOUS MATCHING SHUTTERS WERE A LUCKY FIND—THEY ALL CAME ORIGINALLY FROM THE SAME FRENCH CHATEAU. You can find different types of shutter at antique stores and fairs. It's unlikely that they will be an exact fit, so you may have to get a carpenter to build a frame for them, as here. Alternatively, you could lean them against the wall if you don't want to make them into cupboard doors.

Both these homes use shutters but in different ways. As a backdrop to three orchid plants and a pair of lamps, they create a unique piece of wall art. The run of four shutters is wall art, too, but with a practical purpose—they are also closet doors.

The thick walls of this old cottage, high in the
hills of southwest France, are showing their age
gracefully. SUN-BLEACHED SUMMERS AND THE
PASSING OF TIME HAVE CAUSED THE PLASTER TO
PEEL, MAKING UNUSUAL AND UNEXPECTED PATTERNS
ON THE WALLS. The effect is quite magical, and
how thrilling it is to use the patterns as part
of the wall display.

A variety of individual vintage plates of
different sizes, positioned so that they enhance
the pattern on the worn wall, creates a flow,
which makes the space very pleasing to look at
and totally unique. There is something of a Dutch
still-life painting about it. FOR THIS IDEA TO WORK,
YOU NEED TO CHOOSE A COLOR PALETTE—IN THIS INSTANCE, IT
IS BLUE. Hang up the plates with plate hangers
and overlap them, using a small block of wood
to get them to stand away from the wall. The 3-D
effect created in this way gives more depth to
the display.

THIS IS A VERY CASUAL LIVING SPACE, WITHOUT
A HINT OF FORMALITY, SO PLAYING WITH A BLANK
EXPANSE OF WALL IN THIS WAY SUITS THE
ATMOSPHERE PERFECTLY. It's also enormous fun!
If you tire of the display, something else
catches your eye, or the markings on the wall
change, this random piece of wall art of PLATES
CAN SIMPLY AND QUICKLY BE REPLACED BY SOMETHING ELSE.

Although the sinuous pattern
created by the plates looks quite
random, it is actually imitating the
natural markings on the plaster wall
caused by the passing of time. It
creates a remarkably effective
decoration that transforms an
otherwise ordinary wall.

This dining room is testament to how you can make giant leaps when planning or considering a wall space. Placing a large and bold oil painting in a small room with a low ceiling is a daring move, but look at how well it works here. THE IMPOSING CANVAS DEPICTING A VINTAGE GOWN STANDS ALONE, WITHOUT COMPETITION, WHICH MEANS THAT IT CAN BE PROPERLY ENJOYED. It is almost like having an extra person at the table. The charming, simple setting uses a limited palette of colors, and nothing shouts or conflicts with anything else. THE OVERALL EFFECT IS ONE OF BALANCE AND REFINED TASTE.

The only other decorative piece in the room is the opulent crystal chandelier with arms of black metal. Hanging centrally over the dining table, it gives the room a sense of grandeur and sophistication. In this picture, the table is bare, except for a plain white tablecloth. When it is set for formal dining with candles, flowers, and crystal glasses, it takes on a completely different look but even then the painting is still the most important feature in the room. The French dining chairs with linen upholstery balance the dining experience perfectly.

A large oil painting on canvas of a vintage gown makes a profound statement by the artist as well as the owner. It expresses their mutual love of beautiful, exquisite gowns and recalls a lifetime spent surrounded by them.

The sparkling whites of the brick wall tiles and the roll-top bath, combined with natural materials and grouped collectibles, give this bathroom the feel of an idyllic retreat.

SEASHELLS ARE OFTEN CONSIDERED THE PERFECT ACCESSORY FOR THE BATHROOM, BUT USED UNIMAGINATIVELY THEY CAN BE A DECORATIVE CLICHÉ. That, most definitely, is not the case here. THE EXQUISITE FAN OF CORAL PROTECTED UNDER GLASS, AND A COLLAGE OF SHELLS, STARFISH, AND SAND SET BEHIND A BATTERED ANTIQUE FRAME ARE GLORIOUS ARTWORKS. On either side are antique train luggage racks, an inspired choice for storing towels.

The vintage bathroom stand is a real find. A tall chrome shaving mirror runs through the center of the wooden table. Attached to it are brushed-steel bowls for shaving foam and water. Candles fixed to the mirror hint at the age of the piece.

A tranquil bathroom space with distinctive artwork displaying sea treasures, such as coral, tiny pebbles, and starfish. Antique train luggage racks are an inspired but practical solution for storing fine cotton towels and hanging shiny mother-of-pearl shells.

Clear acrylic boxes of different sizes, piled high in an irregular pattern, make a bespoke display case for a variety of treasured objects. As the boxes are easy to move around, changing their contents is quickly and simply done.

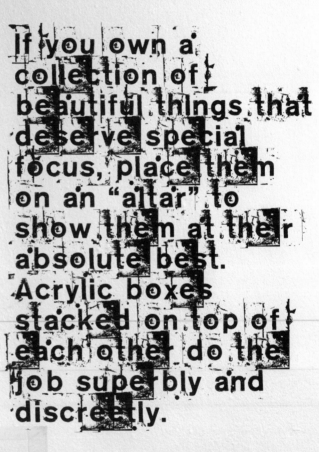

If you own a collection of beautiful things that deserve special focus, place them on an "altar" to show them at their absolute best. Acrylic boxes stacked on top of each other do the job superbly and discreetly.

Driftwood provides the most natural art. Hanging from hooks in the wall and randomly placed, these organic forms take on a life of their own. This breathtaking display costs next to nothing to create, and is so easy to do.

The owners of this grand country house are in constant pursuit of outstanding rare and exotic pieces for their quirky collections. Their living room is the harbinger of things to come—there are examples of taxidermy, animal skulls, and horns on display in many of the other rooms, too.

Stripped back to its bare bones, this room is traditional through and through, from the deep baseboard (skirting-board) and egg-and-dart cornice to the original stone fireplace. What sets it apart from rooms in other country houses is its unusual decorative style. LOOKED AT INDIVIDUALLY, THE DECORATIVE PIECES DO APPEAR TRADITIONAL IN STYLE, BUT WHEN THE SCENE IS TAKEN AS A WHOLE, SOMETHING ECCENTRIC EMERGES. Stag deer skulls complete with their antlers frame the fireplace, while a pair of perfectly smooth water-buffalo horns lies sinuously on the mantelshelf. EITHER SIDE, STUFFED BIRDS IN DISPLAY CASES ARE PILED HIGH WITH OTHER QUIRKY OBJECTS. The rather somber, aristocratic Countess Desmond in the oil painting seems bemused by the whole thing.

In true country-house style, the room appears symmetrical but you soon realize that, except for the two gilt-edged armchairs, the symmetry is slightly skewed-the pillar candlestick is paired with an unusual floor lamp, for example, and the two taxidermy display cases are different in size. IT REALLY SHOULDN'T COME AS A HUGE SURPRISE TO LEARN THAT THE COUPLE WHO HAVE PRODUCED THIS UNIQUE AND ORIGINAL TWIST ON THE COUNTRY-HOUSE STYLE ARE FAR FROM BEING TRADITIONAL AND OLD-FASHIONED—THEY ARE YOUNG AND CREATIVE, AND WORK IN THE WORLD OF FASHION.

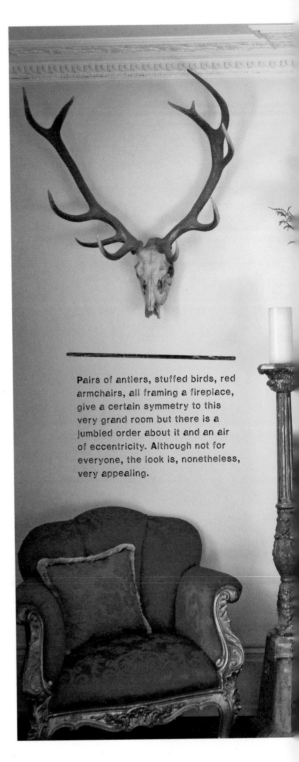

Pairs of antlers, stuffed birds, red armchairs, all framing a fireplace, give a certain symmetry to this very grand room but there is a jumbled order about it and an air of eccentricity. Although not for everyone, the look is, nonetheless, very appealing.

An unusual choice of decoration, including rare animal horns and a stuffed swan, create a certain symmetry over the drinks tray in the dining room. Pairs of decorative items, such as the ironwork sconces, give an opportunity to balance a scene.

◄◄ The historic virtue of these walls remains intact. Over time, different layers of color and texture have emerged, resulting in a stunning marbled finish that is mesmerizing to look at. The stuffed baby crocodile on the mantelshelf displays similar colors.

The marbled effect of the walls makes a distinctive backdrop for the candle sconce and exotic beaded flowers. Displayed in vases filled with tiny white pebbles, the flowers bring a certain softness to a predominantly formal setting.

If you have a passion, indulge it. A love of taxidermy is very apparent here and the various stuffed animals make a strong initial impact. They excite and intrigue at the same time which I believe is exactly what the owners wanted.

←◀ Although the displays of stuffed animals, skulls, and horns, along with the distressed patina of the walls, achieve a museum-like effect, the room is pristine and ordered, not dusty and chaotic. Life can continue comfortably and happily among them.

So dramatic is the effect of the stuffed baby crocodile on the wall that it makes you almost question whether it is actually alive and moving! The gilt frame of the painting blends perfectly with the setting.

A window, where the light comes flooding in, is the perfect frame to showcase almost anything. It becomes part of a painting and integral to the decoration of a room. IF YOU USE A WINDOW TO FRAME SOMETHING OF INTEREST LIKE THE GARDEN BEYOND, RATHER THAN HIDE IT, THE ROOM LOOKS BIGGER. LEFT BARE, A WINDOW LETS IN MORE LIGHT, WHICH IS PARTICULARLY IMPORTANT FOR THE WALLS AND THE ART THAT HANGS ON THEM.

Somewhat incongruously, a shark's jaw hangs from the window clasp. It is the focus of this living-room window scene, and has become a real talking point among visitors. Although the window is bare, the original wooden shutters can be pulled across for privacy or for warmth, should the need arise. THE WINDOW IS A LOVELY BACKDROP FOR THE CURVACEOUS ANTIQUE SOFA, CREATING A DRAMATIC AND BEGUILING LIVING SPACE.

In the entrance hall, a selection of naturally shed horns hang from the top of the window frame. A vase of vibrant flowers brings much needed color to this earthy environment, and hints to guests at the dramatic style of decoration beyond.

↑ ←← Bare windows have become pieces of art in their own right. Here, they have been used to frame a view of trees and grasses outside and for hanging horns and bones, as well highlighting a colorful flower arrangement.

THIS SPACE IS ALMOST LIKE A FILM SET—DRAMATIC AND INTRIGUING. Even though the walls, the backdrop, have been restored and are free of damp and decay, they hold onto the character that comes with their age.

YOU NEED TO BE CONFIDENT AND CLEVER TO CREATE A STYLE LIKE THIS AND THEN LIVE WITH IT. FROM THE START, THE OWNERS WERE WILLING TO GET THE MOST FROM THE HISTORY OF THEIR HOUSE, WHICH HAD OBVIOUSLY LIVED A FULL LIFE, revealed through the layers of paint and paper that have been stripped back from the walls. In this reception room, the nature theme continues with more animal skulls, and strings of shells hang from one side of the pelmet like a curtain for yet another unique decorating twist.

THE COUPLE HAVE WORKED HARD TO FILL THE SPACE WITH A WEALTH OF UNUSUAL OBJECTS, AND THEY HAVE SUCCEEDED IN PULLING TOGETHER A POWERFUL VISUAL FEAST. The work continues, however. This is a lifelong project for them, and one that takes diligence and perseverance, as well as a profound love of the hunt.

↑ ➡ The skull of a ram with magnificent curly horns, dripping wax candles on the candelabra, and the porcelain statue of the head of their dog Desmond—all these elements have a strong individual style and work together with clear authority.

What a clever way to display your
jewelry! Line an old frame with felt
the same color as the wall, and pin

your pieces to it. You then have
a cool piece of art, and it's easy
to choose what to wear.

The focus of this home office in a converted barn is the memory board of concert tickets, made out of four industrial metal frames. The wood-paneled wall is in stark contrast to the thick stone walls elsewhere in this French home, and is evidence of how the owners enjoy living among contrasting styles. Many design features have been added to the barn, including the recess in the room beyond, which houses a statue of the Hindu god Ganesha, brought back from a trip to India.

The band of choice back in the early **1980s** appears to have been Japan. Although the tickets on display are mainly for music concerts, you'll also notice less mainstream events such as the Alternative Miss World contest that took place in **1986**.

Four old industrial metal frames, which had been discarded by an antiques dealer at the end of a fair and picked up by the owners, were the inspiration behind the display of concert tickets. ALTHOUGH THE COUPLE CAME ACROSS THE FRAMES BY ACCIDENT, THEY VIEWED THEM WITH AN OPEN MIND AND WERE ABLE TO VISUALIZE WHAT THEY COULD CREATE WITH THEM AND WHERE IN THEIR HOME THEY COULD PLACE THEM. WHO WOULD HAVE THOUGHT SOMETHING SO WONDERFUL COULD COME OUT OF SUCH A MUNDANE FIND?

Hung in the home office, this clever and unusual memory board has become a point of conversation with every visitor, as well as welcome relief when work starts to overwhelm. It's what I call living art–each ticket tells a story and evokes a memory of a certain time. FOR THOSE OF US WHO LIKE TO HOARD THIS KIND OF MEMORABILIA, IT IS THE PERFECT SOLUTION. I was really surprised at the number of my friends who have saved their

A memory board of concert tickets, shared with the family down the generations, provides an intriguing window into the lives of younger selves.

concert tickets over the years, but most of them have done nothing with them. DISPLAYING YOUR TICKETS FOR OTHERS TO SEE IS HUGELY ENJOYABLE AS YOU SHARE MEMORIES OF THE CONCERTS IN QUESTION AND DISCUSS YOUR CHANGING MUSICAL TASTES.

Making art from tickets couldn't be easier. Each ticket has already been carefully designed in its own right, and all you have to do is find an appropriate frame and arrange them to produce your own idiosyncratic work of art.

At first glance, you could be forgiven for thinking that you've
been transported to an exotic beachside eatery when you enter this
restaurant just outside London. THE CAPTIVATING AMBIANCE HAS BEEN VERY
CLEVERLY RENDERED MAINLY THROUGH THE DIFFERENT TEXTURES, BOTH EXOTIC AND NATURAL,
used to decorate the walls. Split bamboo and coir blinds act as the
backdrop to hanging wool paisley throws and fabrics in muted vegetable
dyes, mixed with a variety of colorful ethnic art depicting sacred
Hindu gods such as Ganesha, the god of wisdom, bearded maharishis, and
sari-clad ladies. WELL-WORN TABLES, WITH THEIR STRIPPED PAINT
SHOWING THE LAYERS OF TIME, AND GARDEN CHAIRS ADD TO THE CASUAL,
RELAXED ATMOSPHERE. Providing splashes of green around the space are
soft tropical ferns in old metal planters, contributing still further
to the calm, almost spiritual feel of the space.

The vintage French metal chairs,
aged with verdigris, balance
the natural shades provided in
this decoration. To add life and
spirit, hot pink shades have
been introduced in the form of
cushions and flowers. The old
ceiling fan evokes a bygone age
in tropical climes.

◄── This retro living room, with perfectly balanced shades of chocolate-brown and tangerine, has used a truly original idea of hanging a deep-pile wool rug on the wall, cleverly pulling all the colors in the space together.

The bedroom in this beautiful modern home has a single wall decorated with wallpaper. Resembling a line drawing, the monochrome pattern of looming trees is very striking and adds a unique dimension to the room. The wooden bird on the bedside table completes the forest theme.

When considering wall art, you cannot ignore Supermarket Sarah, both the person and the brand. After leaving the corporate world, Sarah set up a small store in her own living room in London, using the walls as her selling space. From these pictures, you can see examples of previous walls that she has created for her website. They show **A STUNNING SELECTION OF SECONDHAND CLOTHING, SHOES, BOOTS, HANDBAGS, VINTAGE ORNAMENTS, PHOTOGRAPHS, AND MUCH, MUCH MORE,** gathered together after trips to thrift stores, garage sales, and antique shops in the UK and Scandinavia. Once an item has been sold, it is quickly replaced with something else on the wall. AS WELL AS BEING STORE DISPLAYS, THE WALLS ARE VERY PLEASING TO LOOK AT, AND THEY ILLUSTRATE PERFECTLY THAT YOU NEEDN'T BE TIED BY CONVENTION WHEN IT COMES TO DECORATING YOURS AT HOME.

Sarah's collaborations with many interesting and diverse individuals have exposed her as one of the bright stars in the current competitive world of retail. These three pictures are all examples of walls that she has created for her website, with the items on display probably sold a long time ago and replaced by something new. Crucial to the effectiveness of each display, and to any display you might create at home, is a linking theme, such as color or product type.

Supermarket
SARAH

CLICK ON ITEMS TO BUY

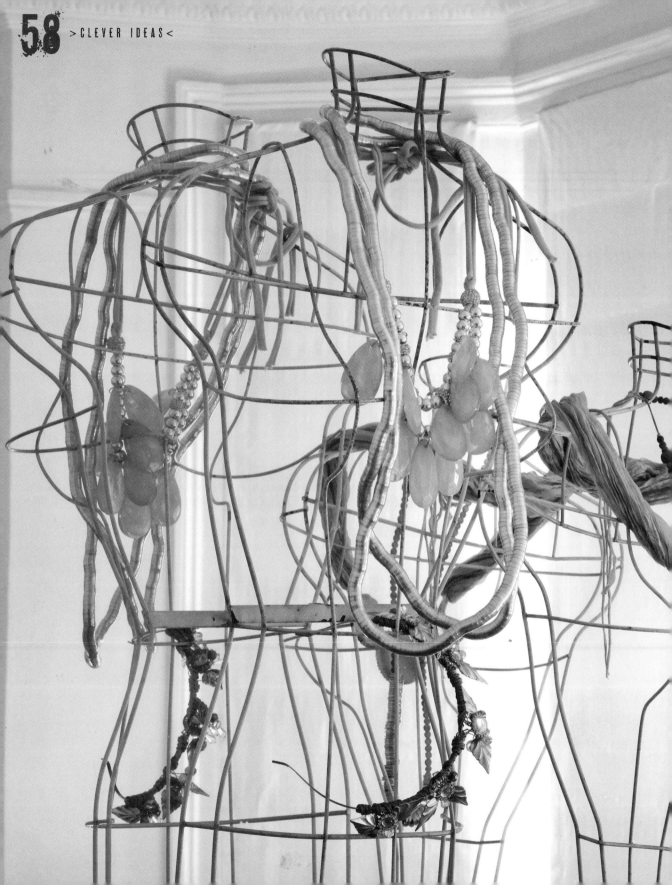

Vintage wire busts on a mantelshelf have a practical purpose—
holding jewelry—as well as a decorative one. The busts, reflected
in the mirror behind, create a unique piece of art. The framed
print alongside illustrates the dramatic effect that can be
achieved by mixing two very different styles of wall decoration.

◄◄ You have a small room and want to make it look bigger? Hanging pictures opposite a large mirror creates a magical illusion. It represents layers of images, making the room appear larger, and creates excitement.

CHAPTER 2
IT'S MAGIC...
creating illusions from art

▲ Hanging a pretty light or decorative chandelier at a low level brings in a multi-dimensional image, enhancing your art and ornaments. Here, hanging a small mirror opposite a large one produces an unusual effect.

This collection of art and photographs was chosen with the room in mind and grouped together for their composition, size, and subject. THEY ARE SPECIFICALLY ARRANGED TO ENHANCE THE INTERIOR DESIGN OF THE ROOM. Dark frames and sepia or black-and-white images, all balanced against the natural linen sofas and worn accessories in a very pure environment, give a SOFT, COMFORTABLE VIBE.

When you look at old family photos, the images may not immediately look right, but imagine them converted to black and white and cropped and enlarged. IT DOESN'T MATTER IF THE IMAGE BECOMES GRAINY, AS THAT ADDS TO THE BEAUTY. Have some framed professionally or put them in OLD FRAMES FROM A THRIFT STORE—IT'S THE MIX THAT MAKES IT SPECIAL. When hanging a group of pictures, first lay them on the floor and move them around to get the right combination (photograph them to remember their order)- in this way you can play around with them until you get it just right.

What better way to enjoy your collection of antique framed butterflies than languishing in a beautiful roll-top bath? With their reflections cast all around, it is easy to appreciate the iridescent colors and patterns of their tissue-paper-thin wings.

A number of mirrors placed around a room can play
havoc with reality as they cast their reflections
and make you question what is real and what is
not. THIS BATHROOM SCENE IS PUZZLING—IT'S NOT IMMEDIATELY
APPARENT WHAT YOU ARE LOOKING AT and from where.
Dotted on three walls is an exquisite collection
of antique boxed butterflies. STARK WHITE
TILES BENEATH AND A CRYSTAL WALL LIGHT ARE
PERFECTLY PLACED TO ACHIEVE AN OVERALL
ENCHANTING LOOK. Even the water pipes above
play their part.

By positioning mirrors strategically, you can
very cleverly bring the outside into your home.
Doing just that in this mountaintop retreat in
the south of France has created a stunning image.
Just look at the breathtaking reflection of the
distant landscape in one of the antique mirrors.
THIS SETTING IS PERFECT. ART AND MIRRORS
HANGING ON THE PALE PINK PLASTER WALL SIT SO
COMFORTABLY WITH THE DESICCATED COLORS OF THE
HYDRANGEAS. THE MUTED GREENS OF THE VINTAGE GLASS
FLAGONS, ALONG WITH THE BOOKS, ADD TO THE HARMONY. When
combined, mirrors and lights are a tour de force.
The double image of the crystal chandelier
contributes to the three-dimensional effect
and it is even more striking at night.

Mirrors and art share this wall space. Perfectly married to the sun-bleached look of the room, the mirrors gently reflect the region and all that's special about it. The overall image is one of peace and tranquility.

A sense of drama is achieved in this hallway with vintage mirrors lining every wall. The effect is disorientating, and it is difficult to fathom the shape and size of the room and where the light is coming from.

Seen here in a hallway and a bathroom of vastly different dimensions in separate homes, mirrors of contrasting styles and sizes add space and capture light. THE ANCIENT STONE WALLS IN THE WINDOWLESS HALLWAY OF A FRENCH RUSTIC HOUSE HAVE BEEN TRANSFORMED BY A COLLECTION OF ANTIQUE TARNISHED GILT MIRRORS FROM VARIOUS PERIODS. If you look at the picture of the space on the previous page, you will notice the gorgeous chandelier. Wherever you stand, you can see it reflected in a mirror, casting a soft glow of light akin to candlelight when in use. It fittingly captures the feel of the time when the house was built and creates a welcoming ambience. AS YOU WALK THROUGH THIS HALLWAY, THE LIGHT CONSTANTLY DANCES FROM MIRROR TO MIRROR, GIVING AN OTHERWISE GLOOMY SPACE THE WOW FACTOR.

In contrast, the tiny bathroom beneath the stairs in a London apartment has been opened up with an eclectic selection of small mirrors that give the illusion of space. Collected over the years from different parts of the world, they

◄ Antique mirrors reflect the texture of the ancient stone walls of this rustic hallway, adding light, depth, and interest to a plain windowless space. Arranged in an orderly way, they introduce a certain formality.

↑ The mirrors in this small bathroom suit the size of the space perfectly. They have a decorative as well as a practical purpose, reflecting natural light which is in short supply. Informally positioned, these mirrors of contrasting styles give the room a distinct individuality.

had been long forgotten, hidden away in cupboards. NOW, BROUGHT BACK TO LIFE, THEY HAVE TRANSFORMED THE SPACE. SOME OF THE MIRRORS ARE BEAUTIFULLY BEVELED, SOME ARE SPOTTED WITH AGED MERCURY, WHICH ADDS TO THEIR CHARM. A wash of white paint over the frames gives unity to the collection.

For dramatic effect, do the unexpected and mix candles of contrasting styles and periods. Heavyweight baroque candelabra have been combined with smaller, more modern crystal candlesticks on a mantelshelf in front of a mirror. At night, when the candles are lit, the scene is even more awe-inspiring.

Very traditional baroque candelabra towering over crystal candlesticks immediately give this setting a distinct individuality. The light sconces on the opposite wall are reflected in the mirror, adding to the intrigue that has already been created.

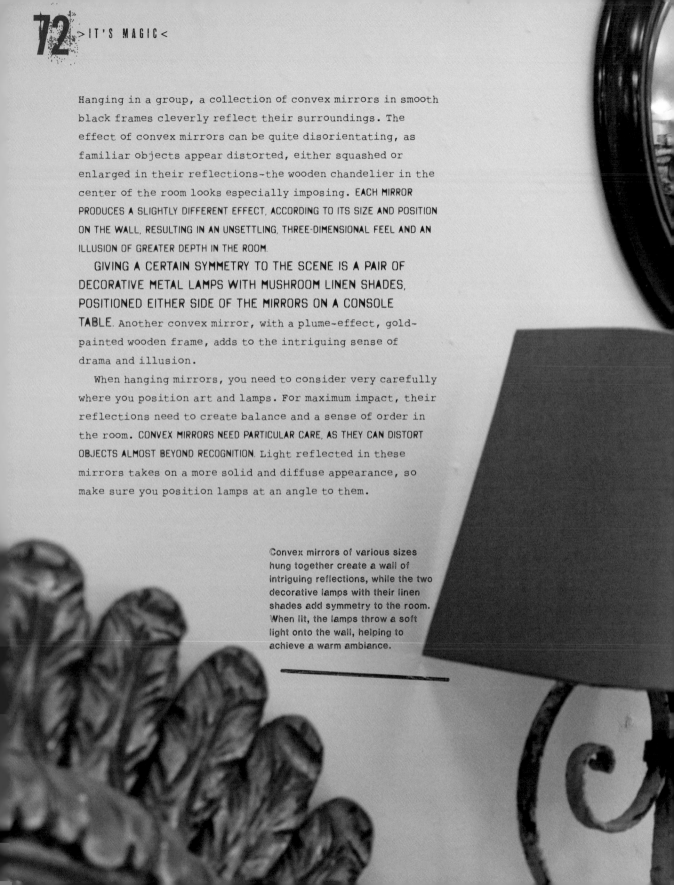

Hanging in a group, a collection of convex mirrors in smooth black frames cleverly reflect their surroundings. The effect of convex mirrors can be quite disorientating, as familiar objects appear distorted, either squashed or enlarged in their reflections-the wooden chandelier in the center of the room looks especially imposing. EACH MIRROR PRODUCES A SLIGHTLY DIFFERENT EFFECT, ACCORDING TO ITS SIZE AND POSITION ON THE WALL, RESULTING IN AN UNSETTLING, THREE-DIMENSIONAL FEEL AND AN ILLUSION OF GREATER DEPTH IN THE ROOM.

GIVING A CERTAIN SYMMETRY TO THE SCENE IS A PAIR OF DECORATIVE METAL LAMPS WITH MUSHROOM LINEN SHADES, POSITIONED EITHER SIDE OF THE MIRRORS ON A CONSOLE TABLE. Another convex mirror, with a plume-effect, gold-painted wooden frame, adds to the intriguing sense of drama and illusion.

When hanging mirrors, you need to consider very carefully where you position art and lamps. For maximum impact, their reflections need to create balance and a sense of order in the room. CONVEX MIRRORS NEED PARTICULAR CARE, AS THEY CAN DISTORT OBJECTS ALMOST BEYOND RECOGNITION. Light reflected in these mirrors takes on a more solid and diffuse appearance, so make sure you position lamps at an angle to them.

Convex mirrors of various sizes hung together create a wall of intriguing reflections, while the two decorative lamps with their linen shades add symmetry to the room. When lit, the lamps throw a soft light onto the wall, helping to achieve a warm ambiance.

Positioned precisely on the wood-paneled walls, these four antique mirrors have a striking effect. The reflection of the silver lamp and luxurious velvet cushion makes a lovely intimate vignette.

Keeping a watchful eye over this charming scene is a framed poster of an Italian Renaissance angel, while the carving of a monk from Thailand offers a different religious perspective. Straw Stetson hats perched on the pair of antlers are a humorous touch.

Mirrors can instantly transform dark and formal spaces. This sophisticated living room is very carefully thought-out, with a focused use of color and decoration, but the four silver-framed antique mirrors are crucial to its success. SPOTTED WITH AGE AND FULL OF CHARACTER, THE MIRRORS LIGHTEN THE SPACE AND GIVE IT A MORE RELAXED FEEL AND LIVED-IN VIBE. The matte-gray, wood-paneled walls are perfectly married with the impressive stone lamp in a similar shade of gray. Shades of gray, from the walls and lamp base to the matching candles, set the tonal scene.

In contrast, this bedroom has a less ordered sense of decoration but it is still very considered in its informality. THERE IS A MIX OF STYLES, WITH WARM WOODS AND STONE THE MAIN MATERIALS. A TOUCH OF HUMOR IS INTRODUCED WITH THE STRAW STETSON HATS HANGING FROM THE ANTLERS, WHILE THE ORANGE RETRO LAMP ADDS PUNCTUATION. Lighting up this careful composition are the south-facing windows reflected in the mirror.

The large master bedroom in this sunny apartment is calm and refined, with a crisp, clean, and well-thought-out appearance. DECORATIVE DETAILS ARE KEPT TO A MINIMUM. Above the bed are a set of three rare Victorian prints of men in period costume, underlined by the white linen headboard. Either side, and in contrast, hang two 1930s fashion plates of men in rather formal suiting. Dark brown, ribbed pottery lamps with stark white linen shades sit either side of

Rare Victorian and 1930s prints in plain black frames, reflected in the enormous mirror, are the focus of this simple but sophisticated bedroom. The frames detract nothing from the pictures themselves, while reflections of the shutters on the glass are a subtle embellishment. The vertical radiator blends almost seamlessly into the white wall.

the bed. SOFTENING THE OVERALL EFFECT IS A BEAUTIFUL WHITE EMBROIDERED BED THROW, TWINKLING WITH TINY MIRRORS. A fallow deer head hung on the wall oversees it all and is a rather humorous touch. The enormous mirror on the wall opposite the bed reflects much of the scene, while THE PICTURES REFLECT THE SHUTTERS AT THE SOUTH-FACING WINDOW.

Plain black frames protect the rare prints and don't get in the way of them telling their stories.

As you can see from the reflection in the flat-screen television, the wall opposite is white and, in complete contrast to the uncompromising and dramatic black wall, it is covered in an eclectic mix of monochrome art and photography.

This collection of very personal
items, each with a deep significance
for the owner, has been gathered
over the years. The pieces share
a common theme of white but
otherwise the display is
idiosyncratic, with carefully chosen
curios, such as coral and a statue
of the Madonna, sharing the kitchen
shelf with everyday china.

CHAPTER 3
COLLECTIBLES...

Most of us collect something. This could be very specific or quite random—it all depends on the individual. You may have a passion for photographs and choose to surround yourself with a particular style or period of photography. Or you may be fascinated by something more diverse, such as certain fabrics, shapes, or colors. WHATEVER YOU COLLECT, EVERY PIECE USUALLY HAS A STORY TO TELL, AND IT IS REALLY IMPORTANT TO DISPLAY THEM ALL WITH CARE AND IN A WAY THAT WILL ENHANCE YOUR LIVING SPACE.

THE COLLECTING BUG OFTEN STARTS SLOWLY AT AN EARLY AGE, PERHAPS HUNTING FOR SEASHELLS ON THE FAMILY'S ANNUAL VACATION, THEN EACH YEAR ADDING TO THE COLLECTION. What started off as a childish pursuit becomes a passion, something to be proud of and shared.

In recent years, auction websites, such as eBay, have helped considerably to feed our collecting habits. We have many more sources at our fingertips, resulting in a much wider choice, but this in turn means that being circumspect about what you collect is even more important.

During the creation of this book, I have met many interesting people who have really impressed and inspired me. They have all approached their collecting with a great deal of thought, care, and consideration. Some have even amassed incredible collections of art and photography, which have moved on from being personal treasures to becoming valuable investments. I hope that the following pages will inspire you to give your collections the care and prominence they deserve, as well as considering alternative ways to display them.

A selection of unique objects in white creates a stunning impact. Even everyday kitchen items look special when grouped together and displayed with care.

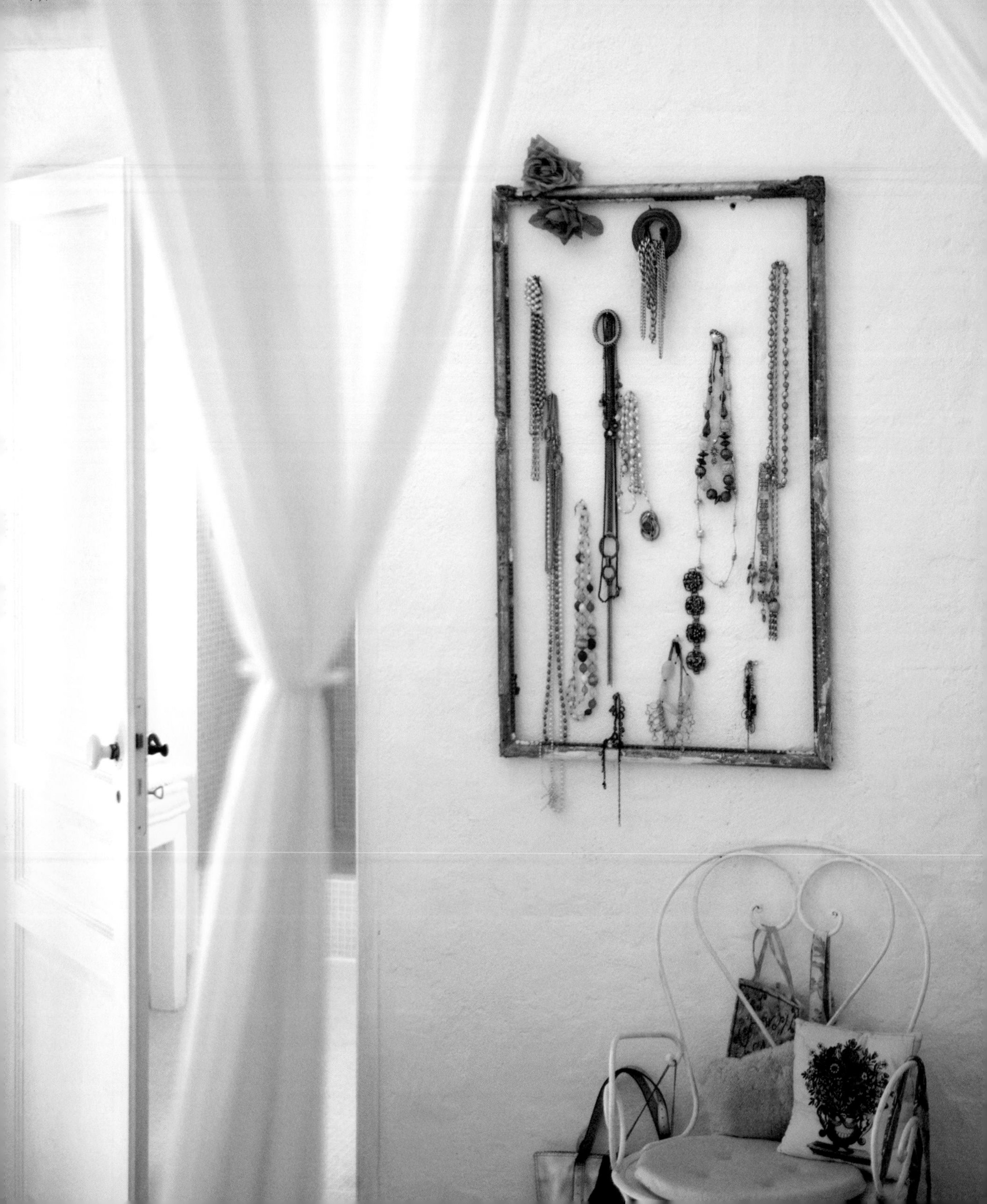

◄🖜 **A** discarded wooden frame
with peeling gilt paint has been
transformed into the perfect
showcase for costume jewelry,
which hangs from discreet nails.
So often, jewelry sits in a drawer,
forgotten and unworn, but by having
it on show, you'll be more inclined
to wear it.

Hooking bags and scarves over
the curlicues of a metal garden
chair not only makes them easily
accessible but also turns them into
part of the bedroom decoration.

Tall, short, narrow, and round, bottles in all shapes, sizes, and colors sit on a windowsill in their final incarnation as decorative objects, cheering up an east-facing window. As the sun rises, the light refracts through the glass, showering the kitchen with a myriad rainbow colors.

This collection of old glass bottles takes us back to a time before the arrival of the convenient but ghastly plastic bottle that now pollutes our planet. DURING THEIR LIFETIMES, THESE BEAUTIFULLY CRAFTED CONTAINERS HAVE BEEN USED OVER AND OVER AGAIN, WITH EACH ONE TELLING ITS OWN STORY.

FAVORITE TIPPLES FROM LOCAL BRASSERIES WERE SEALED IN BY WIRE-SPRUNG CERAMIC STOPPERS AND RUBBER SEALS, CONSUMED, AND THEN RECYCLED. Heavy green glass bottles, produced exclusively for specific vineyards and bearing unique logos and designs, are filled with the heavenly nectar that is wine. Distinctive features, such as raised lettering and bold colors, indicate medicine bottles, while the coffin-shaped bottles with angled necks were reserved for the most dangerous concoctions! COBALT-BLUE BOTTLES, FAVORED BY PHARMACIES AND PERFUMERS, MINGLE WITH BROWN AND ELABORATE CLEAR-GLASS SPECIMENS, TO COMPLETE THE PICTURE.

It's easy to imagine how much pleasure or relief some of these bottles have given to various individuals over the years. What special occasion did that heavy champagne bottle celebrate and how many generations ago? Did that pharmaceutical bottle contain a remedy to ease some poor sufferer's gout? Some of the smaller bottles have a less interesting history-they have simply been dug up from the garden. Discarded long before garbage collections, their usefulness is over but they have been rediscovered as decorative memorabilia.

➤➤ The apparent simplicity of this conservatory display belies how carefully it has been curated. Taking into account color, texture, and material, a simple balance has been achieved, with each object having a story to tell.

◄◄ The same earthy tones and apparent casual order are evident in the entrance hall/dining area, too.

Two distinct interiors, each displaying a keen eye for color, material, and effect. IN THE SUN-FILLED CONSERVATORY, A COLLECTION OF SIMPLE EVERYDAY ITEMS HIGHLIGHTS THE OWNER'S DISCIPLINED EYE AND WELL-TRAINED SENSE OF STYLE. Confidently sitting together on shelves in a seemingly casual arrangement are objects in wood, soapstone, and porcelain, complemented by dried flowers and pieces of coral. Their natural colors fuse together to produce a gentle tonal space, where the light is softened by the handmade linen blinds.

Displayed together, objects with a shared heritage create drama and become a talking point among visitors. The breathing space around the pieces gives extra impact.

◄─☐ Hung as decoration, these cherished souvenirs from a trip to Africa give a distinct exotic feel, while working sympathetically with the natural tones of the room.

A linen-covered Chesterfield sofa sits in front of an original banister. Behind, on a very high floating shelf over the staircase, is a collection of artfully arranged treasures, reflecting the owner's love of natural and neutral tones.

In the hallway, all eyes are on the precious items displayed as the plain floating shelves seem to disappear into the white wall. Carefully arranged by material type, the objects create a soothing and intriguing arrangement. In the living room, the pristine white drawers allow the display to take center stage.

The owners of this home have mastered the art of display. The rooms reflect the understanding and consideration they have given to their surroundings. THEIR VERY WELL-THOUGHT-OUT COLLECTION OF GLOBAL FINDS SITS ALONGSIDE OBJECTS THAT HOLD A DEEP SIGNIFICANCE FOR THEM, ALONG WITH TREASURED GIFTS FROM FRIENDS. NOTHING OF INSIGNIFICANCE TO THE COUPLE GRACES THE SHELVES AND CABINETS. Many pieces represent travels to exotic, far-flung places, where they have searched out the unusual to bring back home. In the living room, strong African carvings sit harmoniously alongside simple shapes of clear glass on a run of white drawers. A well-worn leather chair unifies the scheme, helping to keep the space serene and well ordered. An oriental theme dominates in the hallway.

A stunning collection of Victoriana graces a thoroughly modern kitchen. This is a truly magical image, with the diffused light through the shutters creating dazzling reflections in the table. The antique glass domes have dual roles: protecting and showcasing their precious contents.

The extraordinary photographs in the narrow corridor of this New York apartment are literally cheek by jowl. Of various sizes but all in sepia tones, they are an awe-inspiring sight and absolutely mesmerizing. Visitors find it difficult to walk the length of the corridor without stopping to study them.

Walking into this New York apartment, THE VISITOR IS STRUCK BY THE SHEER QUANTITY OF PHOTOGRAPHS THAT LINE THE WALLS. Mostly panoramic group portraits, the pictures stretch out down the corridor and make it appear even longer.

THE JOURNEY FOR THIS COLLECTOR BEGAN 15 YEARS AGO WITH HER INTEREST IN THE PHOTOGRAPHER GOLDBECK. As the passion intensified, so came the hungry search for more images to add to her collection, with auction websites such as eBay helping to feed the habit. Filling every inch of the corridor walls, and beyond, has been a thoroughly rewarding and thrilling experience for her.

Each image on show tells a specific story and represents another slice of life. THERE ARE FACES TO STARE AT, FUNCTIONS TO RELIVE, PERIODS OF TIME TO PONDER. Starting with photographs of grand American banquets from the 1900s, the owner then moved on to 20th-century military pictures. From there, the collection became more diverse and embraced all sections of society, including factory workers as well as members of high society. IT'S AN ALL-AMERICAN SHOW, IN ALL ITS GUISES.

The collection has been painstakingly put together—there is nothing random about what is on show or where something is placed. THE DETAIL AND ORDER ARE SO IMPRESSIVE THAT IT IS HARD AT FIRST TO TAKE IT ALL IN. EACH ROOM OR WALL HAS BEEN METICULOUSLY THOUGHT OUT, WITH PHOTOGRAPHS OF SIMILAR SUBJECTS OR PERIODS OF TIME CAREFULLY PUT TOGETHER FOR MAXIMUM IMPACT, WHILE MAINTAINING A VERY STRONG ORDER. There is a powerful symmetry to the collections,

Jaw-dropping impact has been achieved in this New York apartment with a dedicated collection of vintage American photographs.

This home is a beautiful mixture of the pristine and very well ordered, combined with the unusual. The real sense of care and love dedicated to the collections is apparent the moment you walk through the door. Wall-to-wall photographs, as well as collections of pottery, art, glass, and more, has made this home absolutely captivating.

too, with all the pictures balancing each other in size. Even narrow strips of wall have been filled. BUT THERE IS MORE TO THESE COLLECTIONS THAN THE QUANTITY OF PHOTOGRAPHS ON DISPLAY. THE COLLECTOR IS PASSIONATE ABOUT THEM AND IT REALLY SHOWS IN THE QUALITY OF THE PICTURES SHE HAS COLLECTED. Along the way, she has discovered a wealth of interesting work by previously unknown photographers, who have captured important or glamorous events of a time gone by, giving the observer a glimpse into another time and a life unknown.

◄◄ A journey through America. This refrigerator in a New York apartment is a conversation piece from top to bottom, where friends gather around to compare notes on the different states and cities visited.

►► Keeping to a particular theme gives a display extra impact. Covering practically the entire door, this magnificent collection of fridge magnets is dedicated to all things Italian.

♥ Retro food mixers form a very ▼ imaginative and original collection lined up on the top of a kitchen cabinet. In soft colors and shiny chrome, all the mixers are in immaculate condition and good working order, so they could be put to good use if necessary.

It is easy to understand why collecting fridge magnets is such a popular pursuit. THEY ARE COLORFUL AND WELL-DESIGNED PIECES OF ART but, above all, they represent happy memories of places visited and adventures enjoyed.

This quirky home contains a feast of bizarre decorative objects. A collection of animal skulls are displayed in a cabinet topped with a beautiful green crystal candelabra. Originally filled with decorative wedding headpieces, the tall glass dome now provides a showcase for stuffed birds. Antler horns grace the walls, while the rather austere lady in the painting looks askance at the scene.

A rather elegant stork presides over a selection of shells on top of a cabinet of stuffed sea birds. The collection is slotted into the wooden shutter-lined recess of the elegant window for maximum dramatic effect.

Two views of the same kitchen show a selection of intriguing objects, including a posy of teddy bear glass eyes, hanging from hooks, creating an eclectic piece of wall art. The vintage brushed steel plate rack is attractive as well as practical.

Peeling back the layers on the wall of this reception room has given it a beautiful patina, which makes a fine backdrop for the museum-like display of rare and unique items.

This room in the same house is testament to the owners' love of individual quirky items. Vintage finds include a model of a steamer, a pile of straw hats, and a carved rocking horse.

Surrounding the imposing, intricately carved Victorian dresser is a very impressive selection of stuffed birds, from ducks to birds of prey, all displayed in their original boxes. EACH BOX HAS A HAND-PAINTED BACKDROP AND CONTAINS AN ENVIRONMENT APPROPRIATE TO ITS SUBJECT, SUCH AS A PIECE OF WOOD TO RESEMBLE A BRANCH. THE MUSEUM-LIKE EFFECT IS DELIBERATE. IT INVITES VISITORS TO PEER AND INSPECT, AS WELL AS ADMIRE. Looking like an intrinsic part of the collection, the dresser, with its selection of crystal decanters and bottles of spirits, is the centerpiece of this reception room.

Creating a collection as impressive as this takes time, effort, patience, and research. The owners have been relentless in their quest, traveling far and wide over a number of years, to build up their collection, but it has paid dividends. THEY HAVE ENDED UP WITH A COLLECTION THAT LOOKS AS IF IT WERE TAILOR-MADE BECAUSE ALL THE BIRDS AND THEIR BOXES COMPLEMENT EACH OTHER SO WELL.

Dark and imposing, this museum-like reception room is an homage to taxidermy and invites close inspection of its resident birds and animals. Grouped together in their original boxes, the birds are truly an impressive sight.

What these two photos of different parts of the same large ?Georgian house have in common is how they make the most of the wall space and create imposing and dramatic vignettes. YOU ARE IN LITTLE DOUBT THAT GREAT CARE AND CONSIDERATION HAVE GONE INTO DISPLAYING TREASURED COLLECTIONS.

The owners bought the collection of antlers whole, and it now hangs with great majesty on the landing wall, illuminated by the skylight. Perched on the large carved cabinet at the top of the stairs is a glass cabinet containing a beautiful stuffed turkey. The forlorn-looking toy donkey, worn out by children over the generations, has a rather different history.

WITHIN THE RECESSED CURVED WALL IN THE LIVING ROOM IS A CLEVERLY COMPOSED VIGNETTE. A DEEP-BUTTONED, SATIN-COVERED, HIGH-BACKED CHAIR WITH THE SPLASH OF A RED SATIN CUSHION PROVIDES GLAMOUR TO THE DARK SPACE. The gap left above the chair has been filled with skulls and horns of various shapes and sizes, which are positioned on the wall with pinpoint accuracy. The top of the recess creates a frame-like

◄◄ The soft curve of the banister and the creaky wooden floorboards on the landing help to make this the perfect wall space for skulls and horns, the trophies of one man's hunting exploits in **1928**.

►►► A mix of the sacred and profane makes a surprising but very successful vignette in this living room recess. The curved arch of the recess creates a frame-like effect and draws the eye to the wall display.

effect, drawing the eye to the display. Perched on a small occasional table sits a glass dome with an owl inside, peeking out at a crocodile jaw. Among all these hunting trophies stands a large, carved religious statue. This might seem a rather incongruous addition but the unexpected mix of objects does work exceedingly well.

Every aspect of this sophisticated room is testament to the
skill and good judgment of its owners. It is disciplined and
ordered, with nothing ill considered or out of place. To achieve
such a well-balanced display of stunning art and photography,
all the pieces were first laid out on the floor and moved around
until the perfect composition was achieved. You can see the
striking opposite wall of this room on page **78**.

Apart from the black abstract flower painting by **Andrea Byrne** and the vertical triptych of crosses painted by the owner, each piece of work on this wall has been carefully framed in varying widths of black or dark wood frames, to give cohesion to the display. The different sizes and subject matter of the pieces, whether art or photography, all balance exceptionally well in this open, monochrome living space. The horse photographs are by **Donna Demari**.

These two contrasting walls are from the same wonderful interiors store in New York. One wall is devoted to the work of the artist Hugo Guinness. HIS BEAUTIFULLY SIMPLE LINOCUTS AND DRAWINGS IN VINTAGE FRAMES, IN DIFFERENT SHAPES AND SIZES, MAKE A HANDSOME AND CHARMING DISPLAY. BENEATH SITS A SELECTION OF TINY METAL ORNAMENTS OF FARM CHARACTERS.

Although it has the same unifying background color, the opposite display has a different quality. It has been created by items drawn from nature, which gives it a living feel. LARGE, EMPTY SEED PODS PROVIDE A PLATFORM FOR DISPLAYING OBJECTS FROM NATURE SUCH AS FAN CORAL AND SEASHELLS, AS WELL AS A CHEEKY, SPOTTED CERAMIC DOG AND PERCHING ORNAMENTAL BIRDS. It is a delightfully humorous and captivating selection of individual collected items, all united by the pods.

↟ This wall display, showcasing work all by the same artist, is striking in its simplicity. The background color almost merges with that of the drawings and linocuts, so nothing detracts from their impact.

➻➤ Inspired by nature, this quirky piece of wall art uses large, empty seed pods as platforms to support each object, as well as uniting the display.

The focus of this picture is the high-gloss, tangerine-colored strip wall cabinet. Although it is functional, concealing DVDs and books behind its doors and also acting as a shelf, its purpose is primarily that of decoration, as a piece of wall art.

This impressive collection of rare and valuable St Louis paperweights, all of them limited editions, has been assembled by the owner over a period of 25 years. WITH THEIR INTRICATE DESIGNS AND BREATHTAKING BEAUTY, THEY ARE UTTERLY DESERVING OF PROMINENT DISPLAY. To achieve this, the owner devised a simple but ingenious display case using transparent acrylic dividers stacked together to create rows of cubbyholes. EACH CUBBYHOLE IS THE PERFECT SIZE FOR A PAPERWEIGHT AND, BEING TRANSPARENT, THEY LET THE PIECES SPEAK FOR THEMSELVES WITHOUT ANY DISTRACTION.

Paperweights as beautiful as these should be viewed from every possible angle in order to be fully appreciated. Here, transparent acrylic dividers have been stacked to form a virtually seamless wall of cubbyholes. Positioned inside the cubbyholes, the paperweights can be easily admired without needing to be handled. Another advantage is that the display case can be set up and dismantled in very little time.

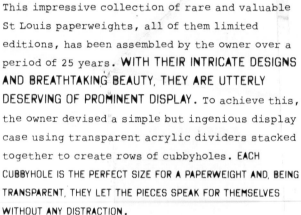

A love of retro art from the **1960s** and **'70s** is immediately apparent from these striking collections of ceramics and glass. By including only objects that she feels passionate about, the owner, with her focused eye for color and detail, has created two very well-curated displays.

CHAPTER 4
MEMORIES

Important to us all, memories come in many shapes and forms, from photographs and postcards to paintings and even handbags! IN THIS CHAPTER, YOU WILL BE INSPIRED TO TAKE A SECOND LOOK AT THESE TREASURED POSSESSIONS AND DISCOVER HOW YOU CAN DISPLAY THEM IN CREATIVE AND ORIGINAL WAYS.

IT'S GOOD TO SHARE HAPPY MEMORIES AND TURN THEM INTO TALKING POINTS WHEN FAMILY AND FRIENDS VISIT YOUR HOME. They remind us of joyous occasions such as weddings, anniversaries, and parties. TAKE A FRESH LOOK AT YOUR FORGOTTEN MEMORABILIA. OPEN BOXES OF OLD PHOTOGRAPHS AND EDIT THEM CAREFULLY UNTIL YOU HAVE WEEDED OUT YOUR FAVORITES. Consider their size, shape, color, and theme and where they might best be placed-some particularly precious family photos you may want to confine to your bedroom, while others you would be all too willing to share with visitors. GO THROUGH ARCHIVED DIGITAL IMAGES ON YOUR COMPUTER, TOO, AND PRINT OUT THOSE THAT ARE SPECIAL TO YOU. It's inexpensive to do, and you can quickly and easily change them for a new look when the time comes.

↙←◄ In this Brooklyn home, ▼ digital images of family, friends, and pets have been printed out and fixed to the chimney breast. The pictures surround the circular mosaic mirror, which acts as a platform for the precious display.

With a backdrop of plain white, this memory wall of photos has created a colorful piece of wall art nestled among a fabulous selection of white porcelain vases, candlesticks, and decorative objects. It has become the focal point of the room.

All these beautiful, precious images are in the kitchen, which is the heart of this relaxed home. THESE PERSONAL MEMORIES ARE WILLINGLY SHARED WITH FRIENDS WHO JOIN THE LONG, LINGERING DINNER PARTIES THAT TAKE PLACE HERE.

A COLLECTION OF ART, INCLUDING PAINTINGS, DRAWINGS, AND A FAMILY PORTRAIT, HAS BEEN PUT TOGETHER IN AN ORDERED WAY TO PRESENT A STRONG VISUAL IMPACT. When mixing pictures, it is important to appreciate that it's all about what you really like because you have to live with your choices each and every day. Choosing tones and colors or textures that sit comfortably together helps you create something aesthetically pleasing but, remember, there are no rules. This photograph will inspire you to be brave with your choices.

Postcards and thank-you cards are tucked into a large mirror that reflects the wall of memory art and leaning bicycle opposite. The painting of the boy is of the owner when he was nine years old, growing up in Singapore—a precious memory indeed. The framed print, picked up at an antiques market, is a rather cheeky but affectionate reminder of a dear friend.

In a New York apartment, one wall is a photomontage of two small children growing up in the city away from their native UK. The parents selected the pictures for display at a major family celebration elsewhere, then mounted and framed them for display here. Although featuring only the children, the wall illustrates the shared journey that the whole family has taken over a period of ten years.

Two different homes show their precious family photographs in contrasting ways. **One collection is presented in dark frames, appearing jumbled but actually very ordered,** while the other is in stark, white frames, hanging in a uniform block. Displaying photographs of family over the generations is like inviting them into your home to share your daily lives.

Two different homes and
two different collections,
both telling the same story.

This homey and comforting collage is in a cozy bedroom of an old country house in France. A MIXTURE OF VINTAGE POSTCARDS, BIRTHDAY, THANK-YOU, AND VALENTINE CARDS, EACH ONE EVOKES HAPPY MEMORIES AND HOLDS SPECIAL MESSAGES. This makes them hard to discard, but it's a shame to just store them away in a box when they can be used to such pleasing effect.

THE POSTCARD WAS CREATED TO COMMUNICATE A MESSAGE OF NO SPECIAL IMPORTANCE, SUCH AS "WISH YOU WERE HERE," AND, INDEED, ANY SHORT NOTE OF GOOD WISHES. CARDS ARE GREAT TO RECEIVE—ANYTHING HANDWRITTEN COMING THROUGH YOUR MAILBOX IS A JOY AND EASES THE PAIN OF THE INEVITABLE BILLS THAT ACCOMPANY THEM.

This wall works particularly well, as the collage takes the theme of the old French postcards and mixes them with retro-style cards sharing the same muted colors and tones. THIS GROUP CONSEQUENTLY BECOMES ONE COMPLETE AND HARMONIOUS PICTURE, complementing perfectly the washstand below and highlighting the subtle tones of the tiles. It would not work so well with harsh colors in this particular setting.

A collage of postcards and greetings cards makes a lovely memory board. The cards are all fixed to the wall with reusable adhesive, so they can be swapped around and added to at will.

Turn your collection of bags into easily accessible art.

You'd be hard pressed to find a woman who doesn't have a collection of bags and baskets that she loves, but so often a newer model comes along and the old favorites become forgotten and neglected, stored away out of sight in a closet.

LIKE PHOTOGRAPHS, THE BAGS HERE BRING BACK MEMORIES. THEY RECALL A TIME, AN OCCASION, A HOLIDAY, A WEDDING, EVEN A CHILD'S FACE WHEN YOUNG! So, to acknowledge their significance, the bags have become art. Hanging from hooks on a vintage painted shelf, they are on show, to be admired but also ready to be used. Their colors and patterns sit together seamlessly, creating an unusual and practical work of art for the bedroom.

A vintage painted shelf has been devoted to a collection of bags that, between them, hold memories of many special occasions. Not only do they enhance the space, they are also conveniently close to hand.

CHAPTER 5
DON'T GET HUNG UP

The following pages will show you how to display your art without having to use a hammer, nails, and picture hooks. Leaning art is both easy and flexible. You can move it regularly to give a different picture center stage. BIG PICTURES CAN SIT BEHIND SMALL ONES, ALLOWING EACH THE OPPORTUNITY TO BE EXPOSED. Adopting a common theme, for example black and white or all wood, helps create a unified look and means that the display becomes totally interchangeable. ALTERNATIVELY, WITH AN ECLECTIC MIX YOU CAN FREQUENTLY MOVE AND CHANGE THE EMPHASIS OF EACH PICTURE, LEANING THEM ON AN EXISTING PIECE OF FURNITURE OR CREATING A PLATFORM FOR THEM, SUCH AS A FLOATING SHELF OR A MANTELSHELF, OR A WINDOWSILL.

LEANING ART CAN BE FORMAL OR CASUAL, DEPENDING ON HOW YOU PLACE YOUR PIECES, BUT IT GENERALLY APPEARS LESS FORMAL THAN HANGING ART. You can create really lovely overlapping effects, where certain parts of the picture are obscured, while others can achieve a mischievous peering effect. Play with groupings of landscapes and portraits. In fact, play is the word to use when working with this style of art display. There is no limit to the number of effects you can create. It's great fun, thoroughly modern, and, above all, very easy.

A rather dark hallway lends itself perfectly to this leaning art. Bespoke open-fronted cupboards, built expressly for collections of magazines, are the perfect platform for leaning pictures in a narrow space. The pictures are easy to move around, simple to clean, and totally interchangeable.

You can literally start at the floor with leaning art and go almost to the ceiling, propping up pictures on the tops of cupboards. You can also prop up pictures on chairs. THE LOOK NEEDN'T APPLY JUST TO PICTURES. Try box frames containing butterflies or shells, as well as mirrors (full-length ones are very romantic leaning in bedrooms). POSITION PICTURES IN FRONT OF MIRRORS FOR A MULTILAYERED EFFECT.

BLACK-AND-WHITE PICTURES ARE THE EASIEST TO WORK WITH WHEN LAYERING BECAUSE THERE IS ALREADY A COHERENT LOOK but, as always, there are no rules. Use your imagination, look at your pictures carefully, push the boundaries, and create something that is individual and unique only to you.

Choosing similar frames and a common theme—portraits of friends and family, photos, and charcoal sketches—allows you to layer in new acquisitions. Crop pictures with others to accentuate certain characteristics, such as the surprised eyes of this self-portrait.

Leaning pictures can be an easy solution if you're not very good with a hammer and nails. A group of black-and-white pictures in different sizes looks very effective and you can change them around whenever you feel like it, giving different pictures center stage

◄─◄ The suspended white cabinet hanging over the stove is the perfect platform for this collection of worn vintage numbers painted onto tin. Beneath is a clock leaning on the chalkboard. The whole scene is casual but cohesive.

▲ These white-painted numbers most certainly had a functional purpose in their previous life on the scoreboard of an Australian cricket pavilion, and there is even a hole in the tin for hanging them. Their reincarnation in this kitchen as leaning art is inspired.

How intriguing is this picture! In an ultra-modern functional kitchen, a whole group of vintage numbers painted onto tin has been propped up against a textured chalkboard wall above a pure white suspended cabinet. THE OWNER HAS A REAL LOVE OF MONOCHROME—THE THEME OF THE WHOLE APARTMENT IS BLACK AND WHITE—AND IT WAS EXTREMELY CLEVER OF HIM TO VISUALIZE THESE NUMBERS IN SUCH AN ENVIRONMENT, WHERE THEY GIVE A UNIQUE TWIST TO AN OTHERWISE FUNCTIONAL SPACE. When he came across them at an antiques fair, he knew instinctively that they would work really well in his home. Leaning gives you the opportunity to experiment–for the present, the numbers are in the kitchen but they could easily be moved elsewhere to take on a completely different look. The numbers appear to have been placed quite randomly here but one never knows!

A bold antique chest with lots of drawers makes a big statement in this room, but leaning two simply framed prints on top turns it into something much more decorative. THE BIG CHUNKS OF NATURAL SPONGE CONTRIBUTE A SEPARATE TEXTURE TO THE WHOLE SCENE.

SOMETIMES IT IS THE LESS OBVIOUS COMBINATIONS LIKE THIS THAT WORK SO WELL. Play around with the things you have, and move objects and pictures from one place to another. What you once thought looked just right in one position may actually work so much better somewhere else. This chest of drawers may turn out to look superb in the kitchen, where the drawers could be functional, concealing and

◄◄ Two bold prints in natural tones lean against the wall on top of this large, vintage chest, accompanied by two large natural sponges, which contribute to the overall soft effect of the display. All the shades are very complementary, with a snap of color in the stripy mat at the foot of the picture adding a colorful contrast.

giving order to all the kitchen paraphernalia that you can never find room for.

The other picture here shows how ONE BIG PIECE OF DRAMATIC ART, SUCH AS THIS DETAIL OF A RENAISSANCE ANGEL, CAN BECOME THE CENTERPIECE OR ANCHOR FOR EVERYTHING ELSE. LEANING THIS PICTURE AGAINST THE WALL, WITH STRONG FAMILY PHOTOGRAPHS IN FRAMES AT THE FOOT, CREATES BALANCE. The retro 1970s lamp with the rather traditional silk shade gives the space an unexpected sense of design, with the orange color picked out in the collar detail of the angel. On page 75, you can see how the owners often use the antlers as hooks for old straw Stetsons, turning them into a useful as well as an amusing decorative feature.

➡ The tall leaning print of the Italian Renaissance angel, a detail from a larger piece of art, sits boldly among a collection of framed family photographs. The bright orange retro lamp pulls in tones from the print and two of the pictures.

Leaning original pieces of art created from buttons and jewelry shows how a unique piece of decorative art can be created easily and without fuss.

Three quite different frames, recycled to hold interesting pieces of costume jewelry and a collection of buttons, lean against the wall on the hallway table, creating a pretty vignette. Glue fixes the jewelry to the glass of the picture frame, and the buttons to the mirror. The beaded flowers and buttons in the shadow box have been pinned.

These two similar rustic scenes are utterly captivating. Paintings, empty frames, and butterfly boxes lean informally on a decorative garden table in casual disorder, while, in the other photograph, the natural elements in the artworks sit comfortably together.

An old French shutter leans against this glass conservatory, providing the backdrop for the small portrait propped up against it. Sat on the aged green table, the antique print works perfectly with the colors of the distressed furniture and plants.

A vintage mirror provides the anchor for this combination of leaning paintings and drawings. The earthy and natural shades of the art and the urn sit comfortably with the greenery.

An old cupboard that has lost its doors has been turned into an unexpected display case for leaning paintings, drawings, a butterfly box, and decorative accessories.

SPECIAL
DELIVERY

← Leaning against the baseboard (skirting board) of a bedroom, the unusual piece of modern art with its vibrant colors is also a prop for a very contrasting piece of art. Together, they provide a brave set piece.

A mid-20th-century sideboard hosts a collection of leaning retro art. A rather unusual piece of beaded embroidery sits behind a three-dimensional boat scene, all complemented by the dramatic hanging painting of fighting cocks and collections of glass and ceramics.

CHAPTER 6
THEMES, IDEAS, & INSPIRATIONS

If you are like me, in obsessive pursuit of beautiful things and spend all your spare time at antique markets and exhibitions or rummaging in junk stores, it's good to have a focus. DECIDING ON A THEME OF SOMETHING THAT YOU LOVE MEANS YOUR COLLECTING BECOMES MORE CONTROLED. Empty your drawers and cupboards, look through your albums, examine your bulletin board, and invariably a theme will emerge.

I started collecting flower paintings years ago, and here you can see how effective they look hung as a group. THE ENVIRONMENT YOU LIVE IN CAN REFLECT THE THEME. For example, if you live by the coast, boats may be your thing; if you are a city-dweller, skylines may draw your attention. Whatever you love, let it influence your wall.

Unframed oil paintings became my focus, but it could easily be any mixture of mediums: postcards, sketches, or typography. By hanging them together on a plain wall, they will have a far more dramatic effect than if displayed singly.

A natural wall backdrop in this covered outdoor space is the perfect setting for a display of very pretty vintage plates that have been collected over the years. THE PLATES ARE HUNG IN NO PARTICULAR ORDER, WITH SOME OVERLAPPING. Their soft colors complement the battered green bench and the old floral curtain, used here as a tablecloth.

Above the bench hangs a lovely display of vintage plates, united only by their similar tones, and a collection of odd chairs. The kitsch prints hanging together in the corner of this space make a particularly strong image when joined by old Lloyd Loom chairs.

An inspiration wall created by the
owner using favorite images
gathered together over time.
Focusing on blue tones through to
natural, the effect is really dramatic.

These three images are all of the same wall but seen from different angles. The love of all things botanical is immediately apparent. Soft embroidered framed images of various plants, dried flowers in a frame, an old tin with a floral lid, the end of a roll of flowery wallpaper trim, together with flower postcards, paintings, découpage plates, and beaded flowers, create a really beautiful and cohesive wall of art in this bedroom/work space. The colors of the various elements gently complement each other, as with nature itself. The theme is very distinct, and many garden lovers would find researching it both fascinating and enjoyable, browsing through racks of vintage postcards and unearthing old natural history books.

A proud pet sits center stage on a comfortable sofa in this enchanting scene. Like the dogs in the paintings above him, he looks as if he is posing, or perhaps he is simply making the most of being allowed on a normally out-of-bounds sofa!

BEING SO DEEP-ROOTED IN OUR AFFECTIONS, PETS ARE AN OBVIOUS CHOICE WHEN GATHERING ART FOR A THEME. Judging by the wall decoration, the owners obviously love animals, in particular dogs. SHARING THE WALL SPACE AND COMPLEMENTING THE DOGS SO WELL ARE PAINTINGS FROM NATURE—A CLASSIC COMBINATION THAT IS PERFECT FOR THIS HOMEY LIVING ROOM. Pictures of overflowing fruit and flower baskets are all in the warm, soft shades of harvest time. Most of the paintings are theorem art. This traditional American folk art is achieved with the aid of stencils formed from a line drawing, and is often created on velvet or silk. It was particularly popular between 1810 and 1860. The needlepoint cushions on the sofa continue the nature theme.

Nineteenth-century art, pictures of dogs, and flower and fruit arrangements, in soft browns, burnt oranges, and greens, sit harmoniously together on the wall. The potted plant and the raw wood shutters, as well as the pet dog, add to this comfortable and traditional setting.

SAINTE THÉRÈSE DE L'ENFANT-JÉSUS

A collection of softly colored, porcelain religious icons sits serenely on the mantelshelf, with a bold antique oil painting of the Sacred Heart of Jesus given center stage. The wooden, white-painted Christ on the Cross leans against the mantelshelf, giving a less formal feel to the display.

A marble mantelshelf with a large ornate mirror provides the setting for these religious icons and art. An ornate chandelier, reflected in the mirror, adds to the decorative ensemble. Votive candles, which are widely available, enhance the spiritual setting of this living room.

Here, the other half of the mantelshelf on the previous page is shown at night. In a different context, lit only by votive candles, the religious iconography has a much more spiritual feel. Another picture of the Sacred Heart of Jesus hangs boldly to the right, while colorful statues of saints, nuns, and Christ are grouped together at the end of the shelf. THE PIECES HAVE BEEN COLLECTED FROM ALL OVER THE WORLD, FROM OLD ANTIQUE SHOPS IN THE CZECH REPUBLIC TO A MARKET JUST OUTSIDE BOSTON.

UNDER MY SKIN

The Style Files

Even though black and white is a striking and easy theme to adopt, it takes discipline to achieve a dramatic look such as this. The extra special novelty here is the addition of red as a highlight, while the white laptop, with a photo of the wall as its screen saver, is an intriguing touch.

Maximum drama has been created from this extensive collection of iconic black-and-white postcards through the splashes of red seen in the vintage Anglepoise lamp and some of the images.

This tree house was built as a
haven dedicated to travel and
adventure, and represents an
amalgam of favorite beach huts and
jungle treks. The walls display an
eclectic mix of African masks, hill-
tribe weavings, Amazonian jewelry,
even blow pipes. Each piece holds
a memory of an exotic place.

It can be difficult to find a home for
souvenirs collected while traveling
but these work very well here,
grouped together. Despite coming
from all over the world, they share
a natural, hand-crafted ethnic feel.

Cherubs, or cherubim, are divine beings, often depicted in Renaissance frescoes, sculptures, and paintings. Classic yet high camp, we associate them with Cupid, love, and romance. The cherubs are very effective in this bathroom, where the white plaster walls give a magical bas-relief effect, especially when viewed from a candlelit bath. Such a scheme would also work well in a bedroom. Cherubs, like most ornamental pieces, look best in groups. Dotted around, they can look disjointed and kitsch instead of fabulous.

The drama of a portrait wall cannot be denied. Hanging on the landing and along the staircase of this home is a disparate collection of portraits. THE FIGURES HAVE NO FAMILY CONNECTION TO THE OWNERS WHATSOEVER—THE PAINTINGS WERE COLLECTED SIMPLY FOR THEIR PAINT QUALITIES OR THEIR COLORS. THEY ARE ALL OILS ON CANVAS AND NOT ONE OF THEM IS FRAMED. Found in antique shops and markets, the portraits inevitably vary in condition but this in no way lessens their impact.

Originally, these portraits may have had frames but displaying them without them gives a certain common balance. We can only guess at the personalities and histories of the subjects because none of them is related to the owners. The mystery surrounding them gives added intrigue to the collection.

Tucked away in a side street in Hove, on England's south coast, this artist's studio is in a run-down yet picturesque stable, part of an 18th-century mews. A SMALL AND INTIMATE SPACE, IT IS COMPLETELY LINED IN PANELS OF WOOD AND PAINTED WHITE. THE PRACTICAL REASON FOR THE SOFT WOOD WALLS IS THAT THEY CAN BE DRILLED WITH SCREWS, WHEREVER NECESSARY OR CONVENIENT, TO ALLOW THE HANGING OF PICTURES AND THE PINNING OF SKETCHES.

As for many artists, postcard collections are an inspiration as well as a convenient aide-mémoire for recalling color combinations,

These three wall panels show different parts of the same studio. The postcards, pinned to the soft wood walls, provide inspiration for the artist. Hanging to the right of them is a group of the artist's own tests for color or texture. A dried seed pod and a piece of driftwood give a sense of what the artist wants to paint, while the swatch card is an illustration of what can be achieved.

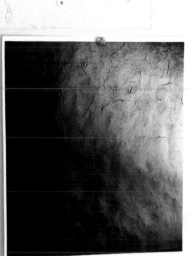

an approach to a piece of work, or even just an attitude. Under the clock, the small picture of an artist at work is a gentle reminder of all those artists over the centuries who have toiled in difficult and uncomfortable environments.

WORKING IN EARTH COLORS, THE ARTIST HAS SMEARED AND NOTED MANY SHADES OF BROWN AND CAREFULLY MIXED EACH WITH A LITTLE WHITE TO SHOW HOW THEY ALL REACT TO A LIGHTENING AGENT. Some colors become much greener, some more golden; some are very intense pigments, while others are delicately transparent.

Black-and-white photographs of revered icons and family and friends make a strong theme for hanging art in this big, sunny apartment. Black frames with white mounts are easy to come by, although not all images will need enhancement with a mount.

BLACK-AND-WHITE PHOTOGRAPHY AS A THEME FOR WALL ART IS DESERVEDLY
POPULAR BECAUSE IT IS EASY TO CREATE SOMETHING QUITE STRIKING WITH IT.
A collection of black-and-white photos and paintings hangs
in this seaside apartment. The subject matter ranges from
the owners' favorite icons taken by famous photographers
to well-loved images of friends and family. THE BALANCE,
FORM, AND SHAPES THAT YOU CREATE ON THE WALL WITH YOUR
PHOTOGRAPHS IS CRUCIAL TO ITS SUCCESS. BIG PICTURES ARE BEST
HUNG CENTRALLY. ALTHOUGH THE DISPLAY HERE APPEARS ORDERED AND
STRAIGHT, THERE IS A SLIGHT RANDOM QUALITY TO IT, WHICH INCREASES THE
APPEAL. This room is suffused with natural light, as you can
see from the reflections of the shutters. Illuminating the
wall, this natural light sets off the art to perfection.

This guest bedroom, with white
walls and simple white bedside
tables provides the perfect blank
canvas for hanging favorite black-
and-white images of icons and
family and friends. The frames,
which are of various sizes, are
grouped strategically together on
one wall for maximum effect.
Natural light pours into the room
from the window opposite, filtered
through the shutters. Reflections
in the glass heighten the display.
The lone cherub above the bed
adds a humorous touch.

It is easy to understand why Audrey Hepburn or Kate Moss could become the theme or subject of an art collection. Even though from different generations, they are both stylish and iconic figures with unique qualities that placed them firmly in the public eye.

This plain white wall in a simple modern kitchen space is an homage to these women. IN THE PARED-DOWN SETTING, TREASURED PHOTOGRAPHS AND LIMITED EDITION POSTERS MAKE UP A VERY SIMPLE FRAMED DISPLAY ABOVE THE WEATHERED GARDEN FURNITURE. For the owner of this London home, who has been involved in the world of popular culture and fashion for most of her life, the pictures of these two famous women are the epitome of style.

As well as sharing the theme of
black and white, these five pieces
of art share the theme of the
owner's favorite female icons.
Although from different generations,
there is a quality about these
women that transcends time, and
their photographs complement
each other perfectly.

This wall is in the same Chelsea kitchen shown on the previous page. Again, the theme is clearly about favorite icons, but this time the focus is on the photographer, David Bailey, who has spent a lifetime photographing fabulous stars.

All these naval theme pictures were discovered at antique markets and fairs. Although they are of various shapes and sizes, and never previously formed part of a collection, their shared subject matter gives them a unity. Ships, portraits of officers, and emblems, all hanging in attractive frames, share the wall in a most orderly fashion.

The seaside theme in this bathroom is as far from a cliché as you can imagine. The old train luggage rack provides storage for the towels, which hang alongside strings of shiny shells.

These pictures are of two different rooms in the same home, which is a treasure-trove of unexpected delights. The owners are avid collectors on a constant quest to find new and interesting items but they do so with a disciplined eye. They are able to PUT TOGETHER POWERFUL THEMES WITHOUT FALLING VICTIM TO RANDOM FINDS THAT HAVE NO REAL FOCUS AND WOULD WEAKEN A DISPLAY.

The image on the left is of a guest bathroom with a strong naval and coastal theme. Filling an entire wall, striking images of ocean liners, navy boats, proud naval officers in uniform, and a beautiful, embroidered naval emblem are the apt and attractive subject matter of this very small space.

The image to the right is of a different view of the bathroom shown on pages 28-9. Here, too, THE WALL ART REVOLVES AROUND WATER, WITH A RESTRAINED THEME OF SEASHORE-COLLECTED ITEMS. The shiny porcelain tiles and the natural cotton towels are set off by strings of shiny mother-of-pearl shells, coral, and natural sponges.

DECIDING WHICH THEMES TO PURSUE IN YOUR HOME IS A SIMPLE MATTER OF EXAMINING WHAT YOUR REAL LOVES ARE. AS YOU DO SO, A COMMON THREAD WILL SUDDENLY EMERGE, PROVIDING YOU WITH THE FOCUS TO GET STARTED!

The drama this picture evokes belies the careful, curated value of the "white" theme. Each item has been chosen simply for its color and for no other reason.

SPITTIN
FLOOR OR WALL
PROHIBIT
BY ORDER OF
STATE BOARD OF HEA

◄◄ This wall in white has been put together by someone with a vivid imagination, prepared to take decorative risks. All sorts of unexpected objects, from rolls of toilet paper to a kitchen colander, create this cool wall.

↑ A white theme can be very simple yet remarkably effective. In this bedroom, a textured oil on canvas and a white Anglepoise lamp sit side by side with stark painted floorboards.

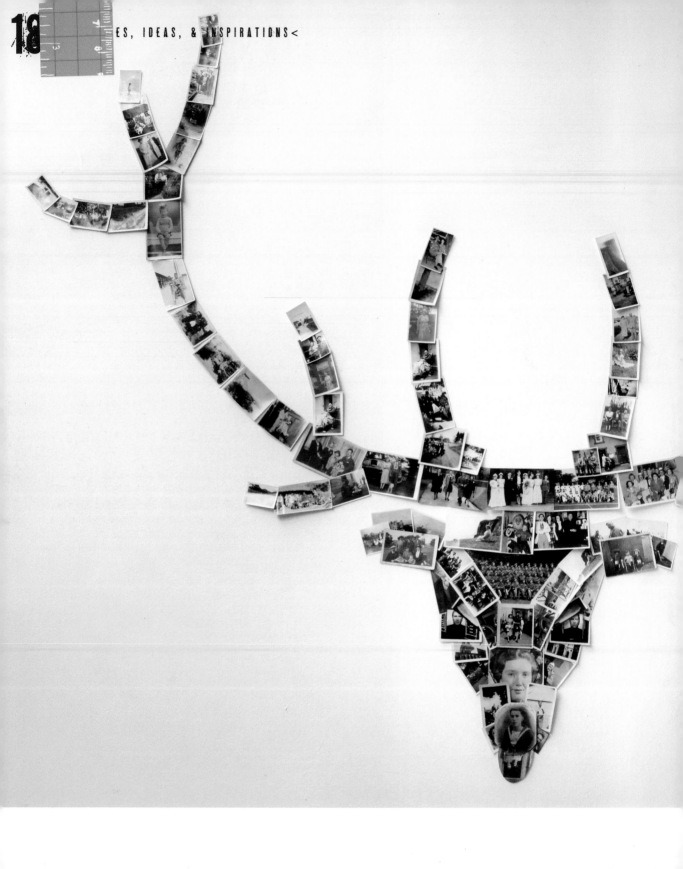

The reason behind displaying these family photographs in the shape of a stag's head was because of its association with the Seaforth Highlanders. It forms part of the emblem of this regiment, originally from Ross-shire in northern Scotland, in which the owner's father served.

➤➤ This shows another part of the kitchen featured on pages 104–5. Antlers and horns are the unifying theme.

These photographs, cleverly assembled to resemble a stag's head, were found in a battered old suitcase bequeathed to the owner by his two Scottish uncles. The collection of sepia and black-and-white prints belonged to his father and they had not seen the light of day since his death many years previously. All of them were taken between 1930 and 1950, and many are of foreign lands–Shanghai, Hong Kong, and Egypt–where his father had served in the army. Others are simply of his Scottish relatives.

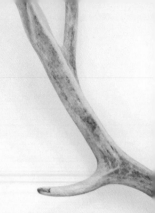

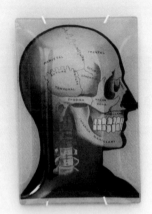

Displayed together, these découpage plates by John Derian, the New York-based artist, have a slightly sinister appeal. The leafless tree, the skulls, the large beetle, and the black bird, have a dark and mysterious quality about them, which is reinforced when you see them together. In this context, the advert for the Devil's Toboggan Slide takes on ominous overtones. Completing the study are two antique bottles, which you immediately think once held poison, two hammers, and a pair of antlers. Macabre, maybe, but truly compelling.

A slightly macabre scene made up of decoupage plates, combined with a pair of antlers, two old bottles, and two hammers.

MAYBE HAVING ART IN THE KITCHEN ISN'T SOMETHING YOU WOULD EVEN THINK ABOUT, BUT THIS ROOM IS OFTEN THE FOCAL POINT OF A HOME, WHERE A LOT OF TIME IS SPENT AROUND THE TABLE RELAXING WITH FRIENDS AND FAMILY. FOR THAT REASON, IT IS GOOD TO HAVE INTERESTING AND BEAUTIFUL POSSESSIONS ON SHOW FOR EVERYONE TO ENJOY.

Natural earth tones-faded golds, browns, stone, and wood-are the theme on this kitchen wall. It is a diverse collection, with most of the pictures discovered at antique markets or art fairs, but the shared tonal theme means that they hang very naturally together. A chest stands beneath the display holding more decorative items that complement the wall: a stone picture frame, two soapstone bowls, an old teapot from Morocco, and a beautiful carved pot containing some dried hydrangeas. The natural wood floors and white paintwork make the perfect, harmonious setting.

A three-dimensional effect has been given to the wall display with the box of butterflies and the carved horse's head hanging inside an empty frame. The battered old mirror with its ornate, embossed decoration also contributes.

Natural earth tones are the theme for this room, previously shown from another angle on page **22**. Above a simple, modern gas fire hang three nude sketches; the fourth sits on the floor. The beautiful linen-covered chair in the foreground and the worn shutter continue the tonal theme.

Down a narrow strip of wall in the hallway, alongside the bookshelf, is an appropriately placed piece of art made up of vintage paperback covers, providing a vibrant theme in an otherwise muted space.

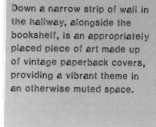

CHAPTER 7
CHILDREN'S & STUDENTS' SPACES

"What should I do with my child's bedroom?" is a question often asked by parents but actually the answer couldn't be easier, simply because CHILDREN CONSTANTLY CREATE THEIR OWN DECORATIVE MATERIAL THAT CAN BE USED AND UPDATED AS THEY GET OLDER AND BECOME MORE SOPHISTICATED. THEIR ORIGINAL DRAWINGS AND PAINTINGS, PHOTOGRAPHS OF SPORTING AND ACADEMIC ACHIEVEMENTS AND PARTIES-the list is endless-can all be displayed.

In seven-year-old Evie's bedroom, an entire wall is covered in framed photographs of family friends, self-portraits, parties, and gifts from grandparents and godparents. The display is not only deeply personal but also very attractive and creative.

These close-ups are of the wall shown on the previous page. Photographs of family and memorable occasions have been given a funky look using a graphics editing program. Cherished toys are displayed in box frames, while christening gifts have been mounted and framed.

WHEN EMBARKING ON THE ADVENTURE OF CREATING WALL ART FOR A CHILD'S BEDROOM, FIRST GATHER TOGETHER WITH THEM ALL THE PHOTOS THEY LOVE THE BEST. Then move on to certificates of achievement, the favorite artworks they've created, and precious toys or special possessions that may need the protection of a shadow box. DIG AROUND IN CLOSETS AND PULL OUT THOSE DEARLY LOVED (AND SUITABLE) ITEMS THAT DESERVE TO BE SEEN BUT UP UNTIL NOW HAVEN'T HAD A HOME.

FOR THE WALL ART IN A CHILD'S ROOM TO REALLY WORK, IT NEEDS TO BE COLLABORATIVE. Put aside some time when you can sit down with them and encourage them to choose their favorite things, while steering them discreetly in a direction that you would like them to go. YOUNG CHILDREN, IN PARTICULAR, WILL PROBABLY SOON TIRE OF THE TASK BUT THEY WILL COME BACK TO IT. Photographs of parents and grandparents, family pets, friends, and favorite teachers can all be considered, while special events, such as school plays, and fancy-dress parties can provide the most entertaining images.

Once your child has made their choice, start collecting suitable frames. These don't have to be expensive, nor any particular color-mixing and matching can be very effective. ABOVE ALL, THE WALL ART NEEDS TO BE FUN, EYE-CATCHING, AND REPRESENTATIVE OF THE SPIRIT OF YOUR CHILD. It is something they will be proud of and will want to share with others. Add a chalkboard to the mix for conveying messages, reminders, and thoughts for the day.

This room could easily be mistaken for a teenager's bedroom but it is, in fact, a den belonging to two middle-aged teenagers. The retro punk wall, with its iconic artwork, pays homage to a movement that was clearly very influential and evokes memories of a carefree, anarchic time.

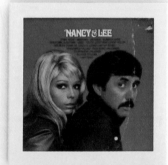

Vintage album covers of female icons provide the art for this wall. The specifically designed frames allow the covers to be changed really easily as and when a new favorite set of musical pin-ups is established.

Be abstract with
paint. This cool
New York studio of
the Scottish-born
artist Lek Braes
is the epitome of
a truly inspiring
work space

For what tomorrow, will be, no one knows ?

Victor Hugo

A striking piece of art sits amid the chaotic and creative scene of a renowned artist's studio. Vibrant strokes of paint left on walls from previous paintings give the studio a dramatic and inspiring feel. Teenagers or art students may be inspired to express themselves in a similar way.

Sun — Alice Party — emily
mon — Shellies.
28 Back Thursday
for
Dinner @
Lois!

henry
sanson

Two old tailor's dummies, one covered in linen
and decorated with a big, blowsy paper flower,
the other painted black, are simple but effective
props in this teenager's bedroom. Together with
the black-painted wall, they are powerful but
beautiful expressions of her personality.

➤ In this teenager's bedroom, gold letters in different sizes spell out her name and proudly stamp her identity on the space. The vintage crystal chandelier adds a sophisticated touch.

GETTING A TEENAGER TO SHARE YOUR VISION AND AESTHETIC OF WHAT THEIR BEDROOM SHOULD LOOK LIKE IS RARELY EASY. IT'S IMPORTANT FOR THEM TO BE ABLE TO EXPRESS THEMSELVES IN THEIR OWN WAY BUT THIS NEEDN'T MEAN THAT THE LOOK IS OFFENSIVE TO YOU. In this bedroom, a beautiful space has been created, which gently reflects the style of the rest of the home without compromising on the teenager's individuality and sense of style. A SLIGHTLY HAPHAZARD SELECTION OF DIFFERENT-SIZE GOLD LETTERS SPELLS OUT IN NO UNCERTAIN TERMS THIS TEENAGER'S NAME, triumphantly heralding that the space belongs to her. The vintage crystal chandelier adds a dash of charm and glamor. Painted black, the door to the room acts as a chalkboard-dramatic as well as practical.

The wall shown on the previous page is also painted black, which gives a stunning dramatic look to the whole room. Created with her mother's help, THIS SPECIAL SPACE, WHERE THE TEENAGER CAN ENJOY HER PRIVACY IN CAREFULLY CHOSEN SURROUNDINGS, IS THE ENVY OF ALL HER FRIENDS. The room is designed in such a way that it is easy to keep tidy, which was an important factor for the mother. The space is simple, with plenty of room to spread out and study, and even to try on clothes. Natural and pure accessories are an important feature of the home, and also of this room-the bed, for example, is covered with pure linen sheets. Such elements help to give this room an identity and an aesthetic that complement the rest of the home.

Covers of the same magazine grouped together create a unified and colorful piece of wall art that is inexpensive and totally unique

With a shared passion for fashion, the mother and her teenage daughter have decorated this bedroom corner with covers of **Vogue** magazine. Collected over the years by the mother, the covers make a fascinating piece of retro wall art.

Leaning against the wall, a wooden board has been covered from top to toe in a collage of images photographed during a trip to Italy. Restricting the images to letters, words, numbers, and signs, all in sharp colors, makes a unique piece of art for a teenager's bedroom.

Unused.
not
Wanted.
Take me

These individual pieces of framed art have all been created by the owner. The bright and dark colors, and the different textures, forms, and media coexist well in this living/working space.

SERViCiO
DOMiCiLiO

7

Fresas

TCÉTERA

Y TAL

The living/working environment created by this illustrator proudly boasts an abundance of art-a wacky collection of forms and colors. THERE IS A HUMOROUS ASPECT TO MOST OF THE PIECES, WITH REFERENCES AND INFLUENCES FROM A NUMBER OF DIFFERENT SOURCES. USING MANY TEXTURES AND FORMS, THE OWNER WORKS HARD, CONSTANTLY VISUALIZING THE NEXT BIG THING, THE NEXT IDEA, OR SIMPLY THE NEXT ARTWORK. To be in this environment provides him with a constant source of inspiration.

A bright yellow coat, together with the straw fedoras sat on a chair, are personal reminders of the owner who lives as well as works with this collection of unique and individual art.

WHO LOVES THE SUN

CASSIUS CLAY

JAMES LAHEY

SEPTEMBER 23 – OCTOBER 11 2000

Iconic references, such as a **PEZ** candy dispenser, hang next to individually created bold and graphic pieces of art like the giant decorated initial.

of Fractions OT Alternativzifferm Plume ist in drei Stärken und zwei Stilen
OT Brüche verfügbar:

for Windows für Windows, Regular / Italic
Mac OS X, and other Mac OS X, und andere Bold / Bold Italic
OpenType-compatible OpenType-kompatible Advertising / Advertising Italic
systems Systeme

User licences for Plume are available to
buy online now, or contact us for details
of OEM and volume licensing, or to discuss how Plume can be modified to meet
your needs.

Plume Lizenzen für Plume sind online erhält-
Regular / Advertising lich. Für weitere Details über OEM
200pt und Multiuser-Lizenzen wie auch für
Anpassungen an Plume kontaktieren Sie
uns bitte.

Dalton Maag Ltd Dalton Maag Ltda Dalton Maag Dalton Maag is a registered trademark, and DaMa, Plume
Unit 107 Rua Oswaldo Cruz, 73/301 8 Dar Al Shifa St. and Viato are trademarks of Dalton Maag Ltd and may be
245A Coldharbour Lane Sapiranga RS Garden City registered in certain jurisdictions.
London, SW9 8RR 93800 000 Cairo
United Kingdom Brazil Egypt Dalton Maag ist ein eingetragenes Warenzeichen und
Phone +44 20 7924 0633 Phone +55 51 3599 5543 Phone +20 2 2792 7540 DaMa, Plume und Viato sind Warenzeichen von Dalton
info@daltonmaag.com brasil@daltonmaag.com cairo@daltonmaag.com Maag Ltd und sind möglicherweise in verschiedenen
Rechtskreisen gesetzlich eingetragen.

Original series designed by North.

Various pieces of artwork, from the
humorous characters drawn on the
back of a padded envelope to the
neon letters and numbers overlaying
a page of writing, have been
created by the art student whose
room this is. Nestled together above
his desk, they create a unique piece
of wall art.

This highly creative wall uses a
combination of expressive art and
favorite inspirations and collections.

KISS

Snow White Lives in a Counc
2

The assembled funky clothes on
the rail and the spectacular pieces
of art that hang together with real
authority speak volumes about
the creative nature of the student
who has made this room his own.
The Pluto hat adds humor to the
unique vibe.

Lots of interesting colorful works of art and experimental processes of creativity are on display in this room. Sitting on top of a desk, alongside a funky red radio, the Ricky Gervais neon sign injects humor.

IT'S IMPORTANT TO ENCOURAGE TEENAGERS TO EXPERIMENT AND BE BRAVE WITH THEIR DECORATIVE CHOICES. HAVING THE CONFIDENCE TO DECORATE THEIR OWN LIVING SPACE COMES FROM FEELING ABLE TO EXPRESS THEMSELVES IN A WAY THAT SAYS WHO THEY ARE AND WHAT THEY LIKE. To the right, you can see how an art student has put her creative stamp on her room with this dazzling neon wall art, created with sheets of neon card in different colors, and decorated with a seemingly random mixture of plastic letters, postcards, old frames, and jewelry. It is a bold statement but lively and fun. THE NOVELTY STICKY TAPE USED TO HOLD THINGS IN PLACE BECOMES PART OF THE ARTWORK, ADDING TO ITS HAPHAZARD NATURE.

The blue neon Ricky Gervais sign in the picture on the left gives an almost cartoon nature to the space, where a fun, naive illustration sits juxtaposed with black-and-white postcards illustrating abstract thought processes of type and image. Again, it is a fun and original statement.

▷▶ Created from neon card, this piece of original wall art, with its dazzling and reflective qualities, makes a fun and unusual backdrop to a creative work environment.

AUTHOR'S ACKNOWLEDGMENTS

I'm extremely grateful to the many friends who allowed me access to their homes, sometimes
at short notice, often at inconvenient moments, as I bustled in with my camera demanding,
obscurely, "I need to take your wall!"—I couldn't have done it without you.

Pages 202, 203: Art Vinyl.

Pages 56, 57: photographed and created
by Sarah Bagner @ Supermarket Sarah.

Pages 10 (left), 16, 17, 187: Kris
Bones.

Pages 204, 205: Lex Braes; photographs
by Rick Haylor.

Page 188: Bill Christie.

Pages 24, 25, 32, 33, 46, 47, 48, 49,
50, 51, 64, 65, 66, 67, 68, 70, 71, 84,
85, 86, 87, 134, 135, 170, 171, 172,
173, 200, 201: Paul and Tina Curtin.

Pages 212, 213, 216, 217, 214, 215, 218,
219, 220: Lee Curtis.

Pages 8 (left), 20, 21, 22, 174, 175,
194: Marilyn and Julyan Day.

Pages 72, 73, 116, 117, 144, 145: John
Derian Store, NYC; photographs by Rick
Haylor.

Pages 14, 15, 78, 79, 112, 113, 114,
142, 143: Andrew Egan; photographs by
Rick Haylor.

Pages 12, 13, 88, 89, 132, 158: Zoe
Ellison.

Pages 30, 31, 190, 191: Robert
Falconer.

Pages 162, 163: Bruce and Julia Fogle.

Page 186: Jonathan Grove.

Pages 28, 29, 34, 35, 36, 37, 38, 39,
40, 41, 42, 43, 44, 45, 62, 63, 102,
103, 104, 105, 106, 107, 108, 109, 110,
111, 184, 185, 189: Howard and Liddie
Harrison.

Pages 124, 125, 126, 127, 130, 131: Rick
and Debra Haylor; photographs by Rick
Haylor.

Pages 180, 181, 182, 183: Penny Horne.

Pages 8 (right), 10 (right), 58, 59, 60,
61, 80, 81, 82, 83, 136, 137, 138, 139,
140, 141, 146, 147, 154, 155, 156, 157,
160, 161, 164, 165, 166, 167, 168, 169,
192, 193, 195: Geraldine James.

Pages 120, 121: Michael Johnston.

Pages 88, 90, 91, 206, 207, 208, 209:
Alex Legendre.

Pages 96, 97, 98, 99, 100, 101: Robyn
Meshaw and Ben Indek; photographs by
Rick Haylor.

Page 211: photographs by Jude Morgan,
created by Steven McFee.

Pages 54, 122, 123, 153: Karen Murray.

Pages 18, 19, 75, 76, 77, 92, 93, 145,
176, 177, 178, 179: Richard Nott and
Graham Fraser.

Pages 52, 53, 148, 149, 150, 151:
Petersham Nurseries.

Pages 55, 118, 119: David Richardson
and Debbie Murphy.

Pages 23, 26, 27, 74, 94, 95: Peter and
Anne Rivett.

Pages 1, 6, 128, 129: Richard and Marian
Sanderson.

Pages 196, 197, 198, 199: Evie
Slingsby.

Pages 2, 133: Nick and Anne-Marie
Slingsby.

SPECIAL THANKS

I would like to thank Cindy Richards, Gillian Haslam,
and Sally Powell from Cico Books for all their support and
hard work in making this book a reality, Paul Tilby, for
amazing creative skills, Andrew Wood, for all his help and
encouragement and for producing stunning images, and
Helen Ridge, for making sense of my words when under
intense pressure.

I have to give some special thanks to dear friends who have
gone beyond the call of friendship:

Paul and Tina Curtin (you are both amazing), Lee Curtis who
has been with me from the beginning (you are so cool), Rick
Haylor, for giving up so much time and getting inspiring
images, Sheila Brown, Richard Nott, Graham Fraser, Bill
Christie, Deb Haylor, Rob Falconer, Ashleigh Slater.

My wonderful daughter Rosie, for typing lots of words and
being very supportive of the whole project.

And, finally, to all my friends who are in this book, and
even some who aren't, who have allowed me into their homes
and given me their time or props—I really appreciate it.